Business
Checklists

Marketing & Strategy

Hodder & Stoughton

A MEMBER OF THE HODDER HEADLINE GROUP

Orders; please contact Bookpoint Ltd, 78 Milton Park, Abingdon, Oxon OX14 4TD. Telephone: (44) 01235 400414, Fax: (44) 01235 400454. Lines are open from 9.00–6.00, Monday to Saturday, with a 24 hour message answering service. Email address: orders@bookpoint.co.uk

British Library Cataloguing in Publication Data
A catalogue record for this title is available from the British Library

ISBN 0 340 74290 9

First published 1999
Impression number   10 9 8 7 6 5 4 3 2 1
Year   2005 2004 2003 2002 2001 2000 1999

Typeset by GreenGate Publishing Services, Tonbridge, Kent.
Printed in Great Britain for Hodder and Stoughton Educational, a division of Hodder Headline Plc, 338 Euston Road, London NW1 3BH, by Redwood Books, Trowbridge, Wiltshire

Contents

***in** the Institute
of Management*

F O U N D A T I O N

The mission of the Institute of Management (IM) is to promote the art and science of management.

The Instititue embraces all levels of management from student to chief executive and supports its own Foundation which provides a unique portfolio of services for all managers, enabling them to develop skills and achieve management excellence.

For information on the various levels and benefits of membership, please contact:

Department HS
Institute of Management
Cottingham Road
Corby
Northants NN17 1TT
Tel: 01536 204222
Fax: 01536 201651

Preface

The first Business Checklists were launched by the Institute of Management in 1995. They met with immediate success from managers in all sectors of commerce and industry, and in organisations of all shapes and sizes.

They originated from one simple idea – that managers did not have the time, or indeed the inclination, to plough through heavy tomes of turgid prose in order to unearth the odd nugget or two which might enable them to do their jobs a little better. They also drew their origins from a former series of Checklists by the British Institute of Management which had been successful in the 1970s.

So why are they so successful? Basically because they cut out unnecessary waffle. They express in clear, concise language what managers need to know, and are presented in a consistent format so that it is easy to pick out the bits you want. They have a wide application, outside business as well as inside, and in small or large organisations: introducing a concept or technique, explaining the pros and cons, dos and don'ts, and steps to follow to get you started. They also provide further pointers for those who do have the time, inclination or need to pursue the topic in greater depth.

Updated and revised since their launch, the Business Checklists are here presented for the first time in a series of books which bring them together under broad management functions.

How are the subjects chosen? Not by guesswork or experts who think they know best, but by demand. The Institute's Management Information Centre handles over 50,000 enquiries a year so the Centre's researchers not only have a good idea of what managers are looking for but also how they want it delivered.

Each checklist follows a similar pattern:

MCI Standards

The MCI Management Standards are the underpinning structure for many vocational management qualifications. Each checklist identifies the appropriate subject content of the standards that it meets.

Definition

Clarifies the coverage of the checklist, highlighting both what is and what is not included in its scope.

Advantages and disadvantages

Each checklist highlights the benefits and pitfalls of the topic, providing a quick insight into the experiences of others.

Action checklist

The core of the checklist is the step-by-step sequence, written in jargon-free language and designed to help readers get to grips with a task quickly.

Dos and don'ts

A brief summary of the key items to remember – and to avoid – on each topic.

Useful reading and organisations

Sources of additional information for readers wishing to investigate the topic further.

Thought starters

Some introductory ideas to help readers begin to approach the subject in a practical way.

Although the Business Checklists constitute a wide-ranging, but concise, library of management know-how, we don't pretend – yet – that they are complete. As they are being continually updated and revised, please get in touch with the Institute of Management's Information Centre in Corby if you have suggestions for future editions.

Bob Norton
Head of Information Services
Institute of Management.

Writing a Business Plan

This checklist is designed as an aid to those responsible for constructing a business plan and provides a sequential framework for its compilation. The success of the business plan will depend as much on the clarity and realism of the thought behind it as on how it is expressed and put together.

MCI standards

This checklist has relevance for the MCI Management Standards: Key Roles A and B – Manage Activities and Manage Resources.

Definition

A business plan is not only a requisite for seeking finance from investors, but also an essential document to describe aims and objectives and enable measurement of progress towards achieving them. The business plan provides the means to:

- appraise the present and future of the business
- work out short- and long-term objectives
- establish a framework for action to achieve those objectives.

It consists, essentially, of three elements: the operations plan, the financial plan and the marketing plan.

- The **operations plan** will include supply of raw materials, technological requirements, key processes, resource needs and production and delivery targets.
- The **financial plan** will assess fixed and variable costs and dictate minimum financial requirements.
- The **marketing plan** will cover how market intelligence will be gathered and ensure that the organisation's strategies will meet market needs.

Advantages

Clear business plans:

- form a yardstick by which to measure performance
- are the starting-point for departmental or divisional operational plans
- provide a framework for offering incentives to managers

- demonstrate that the organisation knows where it is going
- form the bridge between the organisation's strategy and what people should actually do
- can assist in attracting major customers, financial assistance and shareholders' support.

Disadvantages

They require:

- detailed thought, research and application
- the clearest expression to stand up against incomprehension and criticism
- honest and realistic appraisal of organisational shortcomings, problems and obstacles, as well as the rosy side
- writing from the reader's point of view, not the writer's
- regular monitoring and modification if appropriate
- acceptance by, not just imposition on, all the key players in the organisation.

Action checklist

Before you start it is often valuable to carry out a SWOT – Strengths, Weaknesses, Opportunities, Threats – analysis of your organisation, or the sector concerned; it will help to provide a keener focus for working out objectives and for drafting the plan. Remember too that the SWOT does not just involve consideration of the past and present; it can include the future especially in terms of markets, customers and technology.

As a general rule the plan should be not more than about 25-30 pages with strongest focus on the management and financial elements. The executive summary should be no more than two pages.

1. Set the context

Describe:

- the background of the business, product or service
- who the customers are and when the business started
- brief summary of past performance
- any key or influential elements which might dictate the success of the product or service.

2. Define the objectives

Develop a list of short-term, specific targets that will help to indicate progress towards longer-term ones. Measurability is important.

Dos and don'ts for writing a business plan

Do

- Keep it short, focused and readable.
- Research the target readership.
- Draft and re-draft to improve it.
- Organise it effectively.
- Consult as widely as appropriate.
- Address fully any possible bones of contention.
- Outline the qualities and skills of the management team.
- Use diagrams and charts for clarity.
- Use the simplest language possible to avoid possible misunderstandings.
- Provide an executive summary.

Don't

- Be too optimistic in estimating income potential or enthusiastic reaction.
- Neglect to point out the 'obvious' benefits of the product or service.
- Use long words, technical jargon and long sentences.
- Make assumptions on the reader's behalf.
- Neglect help from appropriate sources such as accountants or banks.
- Forget who you are writing for.
- Forget the contingency aspects of the plan.

Useful reading

BOOKS

Preparing a business plan: how to lay the right foundations for business success, 2nd ed, Matthew Record, Plymouth: How to Books, 1997

Successful business plans in a week, 2nd ed, Iain Maitland, London: Hodder & Stoughton, 1998

JOURNAL ARTICLES

How to write a great business plan, William A Sahlman, Harvard Business Review, vol 75 no 4, Jul/Aug 1997, pp98–108.

How to write a winning business plan, W Keith Schilit, Business Horizons, Sept–Oct 1987, pp13–22

Thought starters

- What is your main business?
- Who are your main customers?
- What is your main capability?
- How healthy – really – is the current financial situation?
- Whom are you trying to convince?

Preparing a Marketing Plan

This checklist focuses on the standard model of marketing planning endorsed by several writers in the field. The model contains formalised procedures, although the degree to which these are followed will depend on the culture and requirements of the organisation.

The discipline of marketing planning has been widely debated. Depending on their standpoint, academics have defended the standard textbook model or proposed alternative versions. McDonald, one of the principal writers in the field, in his article **Ten barriers to marketing planning**, acknowledges that 'marketing planning is still the most enigmatic of all the problems facing management.'

MCI standards

This checklist has relevance for the MCI Management Standards: Key Role A – Manage Activities.

Definition

'Marketing planning is simply a logical sequence and a series of activities leading to the setting of marketing objectives and the formulation of plans for achieving them.' McDonald, as above.

Advantages of formalised procedures

- They encourage a rational approach to making business decisions.
- Everyone follows the same strategy thus reducing potential conflicts, misunderstandings and operational difficulties.
- They allow senior management to set out marketing strategy while leaving the day-to-day implementation to junior management.
- They help to highlight areas you might otherwise miss.

Disadvantages of formalised procedures

- They form a complex process which needs basic knowledge and skills.
- They are time consuming and therefore costly to construct and follow.
- There is a loss of flexibility for firms composed of small business units.
- They can tend to take over and become an end in themselves.

Action checklist

1. Set strategic objectives

These have been traditionally set by top management although current practice is to employ more democratic processes involving the key stakeholders if not all the staff. They are not usually within the brief of the market planner alone. They must be kept firmly in mind and the strategies and action plans drawn up must be broadly in line with them. The market planning process can't go forward without them. The written plan should include a copy of the strategic objectives and the organisation's mission statement.

2. Carry out a marketing audit

This process enables a company to analyse and understand the environment in which it operates. It is the key to the SWOT analysis, the next stage in the marketing planning process. It is carried out in two parts: the external audit and the internal audit. The external audit should cover the business and economic environment, the market and the competition; this should examine the important trends which have affected and which will be affecting the market and the industry. It also involves searching questions about competitors and customers, now and in the future. The internal audit should concentrate on the planner's own company, its operational efficiency and service effectiveness, its key skills, competences and resources, its products / services and the 'core' business it is in.

3. Carry out a SWOT analysis

This is a summary of the audit under the headings Strengths, Weaknesses, Opportunities and Threats and should be included in the final written plan. Strengths and weaknesses refer to the company and its internal environment while opportunities and threats are external factors over which the company has no control but which it must anticipate, evaluate and try to exploit. Only key data should be included. For further information see the checklist Performing a SWOT Analysis on page 16.

4. Make assumptions

These assumptions are the strategic drivers of the marketing plan and they may relate to economic, technological or competitive factors. Assumptions should be based on accurate information and sensible estimates of what can be achieved in the light of past performance. Sound information is problematic because the pace of change is making the future discontinuous from the past. Coming up with viable and challenging assumptions involves creative, lateral thinking and breaking with the past. Only a few major assumptions should be included in the written plan.

5. Set marketing objectives

This is the central step in the marketing planning process because the setting of achievable and realistic objectives is based on the analysis of the marketing audit, while strategy decisions cannot be made without reference to objectives. Marketing objectives are concerned with which products are to be sold in which markets: it is important not to confuse objectives (what you want to do) with strategies (how you are going to do it). The objectives should be included in the written plan.

6. Estimate expected results

Marketing objectives should be SMART: Specific, Measurable, Achievable, Realistic and Time-tabled. For example, *'to gain a 6% share of the overall market'* or *'to achieve 600 customers by the end of the year'*. Terms such as *'increase'* or *'maximise'* should not be used unless they can be quantified.

7. Generate marketing strategies

These are the broad methods by which the marketing objectives will be achieved and they describe the means of doing so within the required time. They are generally referred to as the marketing mix or as the four Ps: Product – what are its benefits to the customer; Price – how it is priced to attract the right, or the appropriate customer base; Place – who are those customers; Promotion – how may they be reached. They should appear in the written plan.

8. Define programmes

The general strategies must be developed so that they have their own programmes or action plans. The combination of these plans and their relative importance will depend on the company. A large company with several different functions or departments may have several plans covering advertising, sales promotion, pricing and so on. Other companies may have one plan, for example, a product plan embracing all four Ps. Details of the programmes should be included in the written plan.

9. Communicate the plan

Everyone should understand the plan. It is advisable to make a presentation of it rather than to circulate written copies. If the plan is not effectively communicated, it will fail.

10. Measure and review progress

The plan should be monitored as it progresses. Make sure the measures you collect are meaningful to the success of the plan. If circumstances change, it should be revised to take advantage of unforeseen opportunities or to counter unforeseen threats. Details of how this should be done need to be included in the written plan and should relate directly to stages 4–9 above.

Dos and don'ts for marketing planning

Do

- Be clear on the organisation's strategic objectives.
- Adjust the plan to suit the size, culture and circumstances of the organisation.
- Consult on and communicate the plan.
- Be aware that it is a time-consuming exercise.

Don't

- Confuse objectives (what you want to achieve) with strategies (how you are trying to achieve them).
- Neglect to analyse information carefully and spend too long on projecting future markets from historical data.
- Forget the plan is a means to achieve objectives, not a rigid control mechanism.
- Let the planners alter the shape of the objectives.

Useful reading

BOOKS

Successful marketing plans in a week, 2nd ed, Ros Jay, London: Hodder & Stoughton, 1997

Marketing plans: how to prepare them how to use them, 3rd ed, Malcolm H B McDonald, Oxford: Heinemann Professional, 1995

The marketing plan: a practitioner's guide, John Westwood, London: Kogan Page, 1990

The 12 day marketing plan: construct a marketing programme that really works in less than two weeks, James C Makens, Wellingborough: Thorsons, 1989

JOURNAL ARTICLES

Ten barriers to marketing planning, Malcolm H B McDonald, Journal of Marketing Management, vol 5 no 1, Summer 1989, pp1–18

Marketing plans or marketing planning? Laura Cousins, Business Strategy Review, Vol 2 no 2, Summer 1991, pp35–54

Marketing planning: observations on current practices and recent studies, Tom Griffin, European Journal of Marketing, Vol 23 no 12, 1989, pp21–35

Useful addresses

Chartered Institute of Marketing, Moor Hall, Cookham, Maidenhead, Berkshire SL6 9QH, Tel: 01628 427500

The Institute of Management, Cottingham Road, Corby, Northants NN17 1TT, Tel: 01536 204222

Institute of Sales and Marketing Management, 31 Upper George Street, Luton LU1 2RD, Tel: 01582 411130

Marketing Society, 206 Worple Road, London SW20 8PN, Tel: 0181 879 3464

Thought starters

- Is your marketing unsystematic, opportunistic, haphazard or initiative-led?
- Have you set measurable market targets in the past?
- Are your marketing objectives and tactics known and coordinated throughout the organisation?
- Do you really know what your customers think of you?
- Is your market stable, and your market position secure?

Producing a Corporate Mission

This checklist is for senior managers who have the task of establishing a sense of mission within their organisation. This may include implementing a cultural change and writing a mission statement.

MCI standards

This checklist has relevance for the MCI Management Standards: Key Role A – Manage Activities.

Definition

There is a great deal of contradiction in the literature over the differences and similarities of vision and mission. It probably doesn't matter what you call it, or whether you treat them separately or as one and the same. It is the process that is important and this is what this checklist focuses upon.

In this checklist a corporate mission or vision is taken to mean a description of the road ahead. It describes the purpose of the organisation, identifies how an organisation defines success, outlines the strategy that will be followed to achieve success and incorporates the shared values and behaviour that the organisation expects from employees.

The corporate mission may be known as a corporate philosophy, a credo or a set of values. Whatever it is called, it should combine the inspiration of where we are going with the realities of where are we now and how are we going to get there. The process of developing a corporate sense of mission incorporates such techniques as strategic planning, developing a corporate culture, internal communication and empowerment. It involves writing a mission statement and it is from this that appropriate goals and targets can be set for individual business units and departments. A checklist on Strategic Planning begins on page 21.

A mission statement does not create a sense of mission. Employees must feel that they are part of the process and they will respond to a mission statement only if they can understand it, relate to it and own it. Developing a sense of mission is usually more successful if it is viewed as a long term, evolutionary process. However, organisations have developed a mission statement which they have then used to provide the focus to the business. This approach is usually successful only if there has been close consultation with managers as the mission is developed.

Advantages

It is widely believed that an organisation with a sense of mission will out-perform those that don't have one.

A well-produced mission:

- outlines clearly the way ahead for the organisation
- provides information and inspiration to their employees
- identifies the business in which the organisation will be in the future
- provides a definition of success
- provides a living statement which can be translated into goals and objectives at each level of the organisation.

Disadvantages

Missions fail:

- where there is a lack of consensus within the top management team
- where there is a lack of definition
- when communication with employees is ineffective
- where there is a lack of planning and focused implementation.

Action checklist

The process of establishing a mission is a task for the senior management team. It involves a detailed analysis of the strategy and future of the company. Conducting a SWOT analysis of your organisation can be helpful in identifying strengths and opportunities.

1. Create a project team

This may be the complete senior management team in a small organisation, or a working group of a larger management team. The appointment of an external facilitator can assist in the process of reaching a consensus.

2. Gather information

The project team should meet with the all the senior managers and research internal and external information on the current strategy and image of the organisation.

Interviews with the senior management should seek to identify areas of agreement and conflicts in attitudes, opinions and strategic thinking.

Internal views of the organisation should be obtained from a number of influential managers. External opinion can be researched from press files, analysts reports and from the views of customers and suppliers. Compare the two views. Use the acquired information to build a broad picture of the organisation.

The project team should collate this information and prepare a detailed report to present to the senior management team.

3. Build consensus

The senior management team should work to reach a consensus of a clear vision for the organisation. This is where an external facilitator can play an important role. It may help to define direction – a clear declaration of where the management team wants to take the organisation. It constitutes a clear message of the organisation's intentions to all stakeholders.

Barriers which may pose obstacles to the adopted direction should be explored and appropriate steps and responsibilities should be agreed for dealing with those barriers. This is where the team develops an ownership of the mission and takes responsibility for it. Such obstacles may be perceived at the level of resources: they are probably at the level of core competencies, and appropriate staff development may be needed to overcome them.

4. Draft a mission statement

The mission statement should be written by the senior management team as it needs to draw upon the consensus reached on the future of the organisation. The mission statement acts as the guide to the organisation-wide evolution of the corporate sense of mission.

A good mission statement provides:

- a description of the business
- the mission of the organisation
- the broad strategies to be pursued to fulfil the mission
- a summary statement of the values to which the organisation adheres.

They often contain broad statements of aiming to be the best, identify the importance of people, quality and service and emphasise the role of innovation, communication and growth.

Mission statements should be assessed with regard to clarity, succinctness, memorability, believability and a motivational element, and should be revised accordingly. The mission statement should be worded in such a way that all employees can relate to it.

5. Develop action plans and set objectives

Action plans should aim to build on the consensus and commitment developed within the senior management team and to spread it throughout the organisation. Set objectives by asking what needs to be done to realise the mission. Actions should be planned to overcome the major barriers to achieving the vision. This is where the mission process meets with the strategic planning process. Consideration should be given to the way in which the mission is going to be communicated throughout the organisation.

6. Communicate the mission throughout the organisation

The communication process could benefit from workshops, internal newsletters or group meetings. It is important to develop the sense of ownership of the mission throughout the organisation. It is the employees who bring the mission to life.

7. Monitor and review

The development of a sense of mission should be viewed as a long-term process. Introduce mechanisms that allow the views of all stakeholders to be continually monitored. This should give an indication of the spread of the sense of mission, the relevance and understanding of the mission statement, and the degree to which corporate values have cascaded throughout the organisation. Make use of regular group meetings to enhance the philosophy.

Dos and don'ts for producing a mission

Do
- Develop a broad picture of the organisation.
- Listen to the views of all stakeholders.
- Gain an understanding of the existing culture of the organisation.
- Focus on the core activities of the organisation.

Don't
- See this as a quick process.
- Move without a consensus among the senior team.
- See this as a one-off process.

Further reading

BOOKS

101 great mission statements: how the world's leading companies run their businesses, Timothy R V Foster, London: Kogan Page, 1993

Mission and business philosophy: winning employee commitment, Andrew Campbell and Kiran Tawadey, London: Heinemann, 1990

A sense of mission, Andrew Campbell, Marion Devine and David Young, London: Hutchinson, 1990

JOURNAL ARTICLES

Mission analysis: an operational approach, Nigel F Piercy and Neil A Morgan, Long Range Planning, Vol 19 no 3, 1994, pp1–19

Mission impossible? Designing a great mission statement to ignite your plans, Ken Matejka and others, Management Decision, Vol 31 no 4, 1993, pp34–37

Thought starters

- Is there a broad understanding of what the organisation's values are, and where the organisation is going?
- Is each staff contribution recognised as a key part in the mission?
- Do staff know what the mission of the organisation is?

Performing a SWOT Analysis

This checklist is for those carrying out, or participating in, a SWOT analysis, SWOT being the acronym for Strengths Weaknesses Opportunities Threats. It is a simple, popular technique which can be used in preparing or amending plans, in problem solving and decision making, or for making staff generally aware of the need for change. The usefulness of SWOT analysis, however, has recently been questioned and may be seen as an outdated technique.

MCI standards

SWOT analysis has relevance for the MCI Management Standards: Key Role A – Manage Activities.

Definition

SWOT analysis is a general technique which can find suitable applications across diverse management functions and activities, but it is particularly appropriate to the early stages of strategic and marketing planning.

Performing a SWOT analysis involves the generation and recording of the strengths, weaknesses, opportunities, and threats concerning a task, individual, department, or organisation. It is customary for the analysis to take account of internal resources and capabilities (strengths and weakness) and factors external to the organisation (opportunities and threats).

Benefits

SWOT analysis can provide:

- a framework for identifying and analysing strengths, weaknesses, opportunities and threats
- an impetus to analyse a situation and develop suitable strategies and tactics
- a basis for assessing core capabilities and competences
- the evidence for, and cultural key to, change
- a stimulus to participation in a group experience.

Concerns

Hill and Westbrook argue that SWOT analysis is an overview approach which is unsuited to today's diverse and unstable markets. They also suggest that it can be ineffective as a means of analysis because of:

- the generation of long lists
- the use of description, rather than analysis
- a failure to prioritise
- a failure to use it in the later stages of the planning and implementation process.

Action checklist

1. Establish the objectives

The first key step in any management project: be clear on what you are doing and why. The purpose of conducting a SWOT may be wide or narrow, general or specific – anything from getting staff to understand, think about and be more involved in the business, to re-thinking a strategy, or even re-thinking the direction of the business.

2. Select appropriate contributors

Important if the final recommendations are to result from consultation and discussion, not just personal views, however expert.

- Pick a mix of specialist and 'ideas' people with the ability and enthusiasm to contribute.
- Consider how appropriate it would be to mix staff of different grades.
- Think about numbers. 6–10 people may be enough, especially in a SWOT workshop, but up to 25 or 30 can be useful if one of the aims is to get staff to see the need for change.

3. Allocate research and information gathering tasks

Background preparation is a vital stage for the subsequent analysis to be effective, and should be divided among the SWOT participants. This preparation can be carried out in two stages: exploratory, followed by data collection, and detailed, followed by a focused analysis.

- Gathering information on Strengths and Weaknesses should focus on the internal factors of skills, resources and assets, or lack of them.
- Gathering information on Opportunities and Threats should focus on the external factors over which you have little or no control, such as social, market or economic trends.

4. Create a workshop environment

If compiling and recording the SWOT lists takes place in meetings, then do exploit the benefits of workshop sessions. Encourage an atmosphere conducive to the free flow of information and to participants saying what they feel to be appropriate, free from blame. The leader / facilitator has a key role and should allow time for free flow of thought, but not too much. Half an hour is often enough to spend, for example, on Strengths, before moving on. It is important to be specific, evaluative and analytical at the stage of compiling and recording the SWOT lists – mere description is not enough.

5. List Strengths

Strengths can relate to the organisation, to the environment, to public relations and perceptions, to market shares, and to people. 'People' elements include the skills, capabilities and knowledge of staff which can provide a competitive edge, as well as reasons for past successes. Other people strengths include:

- friendly, cooperative and supportive staff
- a staff development and training scheme
- appropriate levels of involvement through delegation and trust.

'Organisation' elements include:

- customer loyalty
- capital investment and a strong balance sheet
- effective cost control programmes
- efficient procedures, systems and well-developed social responsibility.

6. List Weaknesses

This session should not constitute an opportunity to slate the organisation but be an honest appraisal of the way things are. Key questions include:

- What obstacles prevent progress?
- Which elements need strengthening?
- Where are the complaints coming from?
- Are there any real weak links in the chain?

The list for action could include:

- lack of new products or services
- declining market for main product
- poor competitiveness and higher prices
- non-compliance with, or non-awareness of, appropriate legislation
- lack of awareness of mission, objectives and policies
- regular staff absence
- absence of method for monitoring success or failure.

It is not unusual for 'People' problems – poor communication, inadequate leadership, lack of motivation, too little delegation, no trust, the left hand never knowing what the right is doing – to feature among the major weaknesses.

7. List Opportunities

This step is designed to assess the socio-economic, political, environmental and demographic factors, among others, to evaluate the benefits they may bring to the organisation. Examples include:

- the availability of new technology
- new markets
- a new government
- new programmes for training or monitoring quality
- changes in interest rates
- an ageing population
- strengths and weaknesses of competitors.

Bear in mind just how long opportunities might last and how the organisation may take best advantage of them.

8. List Threats

The opposite of Opportunities – all the above may, with a shift of emphasis or perception, have an adverse impact. Other threats may include:

- the level of unemployment
- environmental legislation
- an obsolete product range.

It is important to have a worst-case scenario. Weighing threats against opportunities is not a reason to indulge in pessimism; it is rather a question of considering how possible damage may be limited or eliminated. The same factors may emerge as both a threat and an opportunity, for example, Information Technology. Most external factors are in fact challenges, and whether staff perceive them as opportunities or threats is often a valuable indicator of morale.

9. Evaluate listed ideas against Objectives

With the lists compiled, sort and group facts and ideas in relation to the objectives. It may be necessary for the SWOT participants to select their five most important items from the list in order to gain a wider view. Clarity of objectives is key to this process, as evaluation and elimination will be necessary to cull the wheat from the chaff. Although some aspects may require further information or research, a clear picture should, at this stage, start to emerge in response to the objectives.

10. Carry your findings forward

Make sure that the SWOT analysis is used in subsequent planning. Revisit your findings at suitable time intervals to check that they are still valid.

Useful reading

JOURNAL ARTICLES

SWOT Analysis: it's time for a product recall, Terry Hill and Ray Westbrook, Long Range Planning, vol 30 no 1, February 1997, pp46-52

A framework for analysing service operations, Gabriel R Bitran and Maureen Lojo, European Management Journal, vol 11 no 3, September 1993, pp271-282

It pays to analyse your strengths and weaknesses, Small Business Confidential, no 57, May 1988, pp7-8

TRAINING PACKAGE

Identifying strengths, weaknesses, opportunities and threats, CBT package from Maxim Training Systems, 61 Ship Street, Brighton, BN1 1AE, Tel: 01273 204198

Dos and don'ts for SWOT analysis

Do

- Be analytical and specific.
- Record all thoughts and ideas in stages 5-8.
- Be selective in the final report.
- Choose the right people for the exercise.
- Choose a suitable SWOT leader or facilitator.

Don't

- Try to disguise weaknesses.
- Merely list errors and mistakes.
- Lose sight of external influences and trends.
- Allow the SWOT to become a blame-laying exercise.
- Ignore the outcomes at later stages of the planning process.

Strategic Planning

This checklist is for managers involved in considering the strategic position and direction of their organisation for the first time. It provides a framework of practice to draw on and encourages strategic thinking rather than imposing a sequence of steps to follow.

In the 1990s such is the pace of change, the growth of uncertainty and the diversity of customer expectations that the major risk to survival and success is in not planning. Strategic planning helps you manage the future; if you don't manage the future, the future will manage you.

There are no magic formulas; each organisation will be different. So getting the questions right is crucial to success. This checklist details the questions to address in the strategic planning process and should be read in conjunction with the checklist on Producing a Corporate Mission beginning on page 11.

MCI standards

This checklist has relevance for the MCI Management Standards: Key Role A – Manage Activities.

Definition

Strategic planning goes to the heart of what an organisation does, why it does it, how it does it and where it is going. It is 'a total concept of the whole business involving a framework and process that guides its future' (Napuk). Strategic planning addresses a number of basic questions:

- where are you now?
- how did you get there?
- what business are you in?
- where do you want to be in the future?
- how are you going to get there?

Advantages of planning

Strategic planning will provide the organisation with a framework for:

- understanding the organisation's position in the marketplace
- moving forward with a sense of direction, purpose and urgency

- focusing on key issues such as quality, productivity and customers
- better motivation and communication throughout the organisation
- changing the organisation to deliver required results and profitability.

Requirements of strategic plans

By failing to plan, the organisation will be reactive, vulnerable to threats and closed to opportunities. The strategic plan needs to be:

- **flexible** – adaptable to change, but too much change can cause havoc
- **responsive** – taking account of the market and environmental conditions
- **creative** – to inspire commitment and make the organisation stand out
- **challenging** – but realistic so that people can get to grips with it
- **focused** – clear, defined and understandable to staff and customers.

Action checklist

1. Involve all managers and staff

The planning process should not be restricted merely to contributions from senior representatives; all parts of the organisation should play a part and all staff will have a contribution to make as stakeholders.

2. Where are you now?

This involves an analysis of recent performance to identify the current position of the organisation in relation to its market and industry sector. Questions include:

- what is your current market position in relation to competitors?
- how do customers see you?
- what is your market share?
- what are your strengths (weaknesses) in relation to your competitors?
- are you on an upward or downward curve?

3. How did you get there?

Next it is important to assess the reasons and factors which created this situation, for example:

- what did you do right (wrong) to get there?
- what did you do well (badly)?
- were you in the right place at the right time?
- what was down to market circumstances?
- what was down to good planning, bad planning, or no planning?

4. Examine your corporate identity

Try to gain a clear sense of identity by asking:

- what kind of people are you?
- what kind of values do you have?
- what people strengths (weaknesses) do you have?
- what kind of leadership do you have?
- what kind of morale is present?

It is important to gain a balanced view of the organisation – not just the rosy side. Do not just believe in what you choose to – seek evidence for it; base your future planning on realism.

5. Carry out a SWOT analysis

Summarise your findings from the external and internal audits conducted in steps 2–4 above under the headings of (internal) Strengths and Weaknesses, and (external) Opportunities and Threats. (The previous checklist considered SWOT analysis.)

6. What business are you in?

Question your own marketing literature. Does it convey the purposes for the existence of your organisation? Think of the focus of your organisation – why it is there and what it is there to do. The business you are in is usually expressed in the organisation's mission statement. There is a risk of limiting scope too much in an age of increasing specialisation; equally there is a risk of broadening too far in an age which requires increasing diversification. Don't have such a narrow perspective that you lose opportunities, but be wary of too broad a church, which might lose focus and appeal.

7. Where do you want to go?

Do you want to stay in the same business? Where do you want to be in the future? This involves a vision for the future with objectives whose achievement will lead to attaining that vision. Do you want to expand into new areas? Why? Or give priority to your 'core' area? What is it? Working out where you want the organisation to be in the future means identifying a target destination which will shape all planning and decisions. Destination is usually expressed in terms of a vision statement.

There is some confusion and a good deal of overlap between missions and visions. Whatever distinctions are drawn it is down to senior management to make a clear statement of what business the organisation is in, where the organisation is going, and how it is going to get there. The statement should:

- constitute a clear message to all stakeholders and to the market
- be inspirational but realistic

- be motivating but believable
- be challenging but attainable.

Carry out a reality-check against the picture which emerged from steps 2–6.

8. Establish a time-frame

Visions are usually longer- rather than shorter-term. Although an organisation needs time to change thinking and shift resources, targets are taking on ever tighter time-frames. As a general guide, visions may well take up to 8–10 years to achieve, but the strategic planning process should generate objectives or targets which are achievable within 2–4 years.

9. Set objectives

Direction and destination must be clarified, communicated and agreed upon, and be firm without being so rigid that modification causes failure. Objectives are set by asking what needs to be done to contribute to the realisation of the vision and need to cover aspects of:

- profitability and return on investment
- market share and meeting market needs
- product/service quality and customer service
- growth and public responsibility
- people participation and commitment.

Your objectives may involve some or all of these elements, should lead towards attaining the vision, and should be measurable.

10. How do you get there?

Strategies must account for the organisation's weaknesses and provide the framework to put them right. The focus of the strategy however is on the outside world. Think of levels of empowerment and employee development; take account of plant and equipment and the investment needed; think of flexible control systems and the information that you have available (or not) to make decisions. The SWOT analysis above related to the past and the present; now it is time to apply such questions to the future, both outside the organisation:

- what changes are happening in today's markets?
- what is happening to customers' attitudes and demands?
- what is happening to technology?
- in which market areas will you have the best chance of success?
- what will customers want in the future?
- how will you tackle competitors?

and inside:

- what people skills do you need to develop?
- how can you improve your product(s) or service(s)?
- how can performance be improved to meet demand?
- what critical success factors do you have?
- how will you generate the resources to do all this?

11. Communicate and seek feedback

Communicate details of the emerging plan throughout the organisation. Consultation and feedback are vital to widespread understanding and commitment as well and for hearing threats and opportunities from those who actually do the jobs. Depending on the size of the organisation, the plan must be translated into business / operational plans, marketing plans, financial plans (budgets), project plans and personal development plans.

12. Measure, adapt and renew

The end point of strategic action is the combination of product(s), market(s) and technologies that produce results which realise the vision. The one constant is to stay close to the market – that means continuous change for the organisation and continuous measurement of progress against the plan. Measurement is a key process which can indicate the levels of change and modification needed as the plan adapts to changing technologies and market forces and evolves to embrace new opportunities. Strategic plans need to be rolling plans; 5-year plans need rolling over every three years, 3-year plans every two.

Useful reading

The strategy-led business; step by step strategic planning for your company's future, Kerry Napuk, London: McGraw Hill, 1993
Contemporary strategy analysis: concepts, techniques, applications, Robert M Grant, Oxford: Blackwell Business, 1995
Strategic management, 5th ed, Fred R David, Englewood Cliffs NJ: Prentice Hall, 1995

Useful address

Strategic Planning Society, 17 Portland Place, London W1N 3AF, Tel: 0171 636 7737

Thought starters

- Have you looked at other organisations' strategic plans?
- If so, do they look credible?
- How well do you know your industry/market sector?
- How close are you to your customers?

Strategic Partnering

This checklist describes the planning phases in partnering: the strategic decision to partner, structuring the strategic partnership, and selecting an appropriate partner.

MCI standards

This checklist has relevance for the MCI Management Standards: Key Roles A and B – Manage Activities and Manage Resources.

Definition

Strategic partnering agreements allow organisations to take advantage together of market opportunities and respond to customer needs more efficiently and effectively than they could in isolation. Such agreements may be for defined periods of time, and may be non-exclusive.

'Collaboration is the process by which partners adopt a high level of purposeful cooperation to maintain a trading relationship over time. The relationship is bilateral; both parties have the power to shape its nature and future direction over time.' (Spekman)

Partnering means:

- sharing risk with others and trusting them to act in joint best interests
- a strategic 'fit' between partners so that objectives match and action plans show synergy
- finding complementary skills, competences and resources in partners
- sharing information which may have been privileged or confidential.

Reasons for partnering

- Finding an outlet for excess manufacturing capacity.
- Gaining quicker, low risk access to new markets.
- Strengthening the technological base.
- Achieving the economies of scale of high volume, low cost and mass distribution.
- Overcoming geographic, legal or trade barriers.
- Speeding up new product innovation and introduction.

Where partnering goes wrong

- Strategic fit may be lacking and management styles incompatible.
- As a result of a poor selection process, one partner may emerge to be stronger than the other, or may become an aggressor unable to put aside older, more competitive instincts.
- Implementation problems can arise from a bad match in leadership styles. Although there may appear a good 'fit', traditional control methods may dominate the new interdependence required.
- Fuzzy communication and unclear reporting can lead to dissatisfaction, which creates a lack of trust and confidence in the other party.
- Decision making may slow down because of the need to refer back to 'HQ'.
- All the requirements for a market project are concentrated in one of the partners.
- There is a risk of sacrificing unique, high-value knowledge.

Action checklist – Phase 1: Taking the strategic decision

1. Think carefully about partnering needs

Very few organisations have all the resources or skills to tackle new market opportunities independently and maintain the economies of scale of low cost and high volume for mass distribution. Going it alone can mean high investment, slower response to changing circumstances and an infrastructure which may require dismantling, possibly soon afterwards. On the other hand, partnering may mean sacrificing something unique and hitherto wholly owned.

2. Take account of the changing market-place

Take a good look at your organisation in relation to its industry sector and market position. Gain an understanding of who is emerging as a market leader and why, which market trends are beginning to dominate and which way things may develop in the future. The organisation's stakeholders – suppliers, customers, employees and shareholders – provide an invaluable resource to be tapped in this data-gathering exercise.

Carry out a SWOT analysis and look at how you got where you are. Do you need to invest in your technological base, in your processing capacity, or in new markets? Does market stability – or volatility – make that investment affordable or desirable? Consider what other organisations are doing to compete on innovation, service and value for the customer.

3. Determine where you want to be in the future

This may well mean re-thinking the business you are in or adjusting your business focus to concentrate on your core strengths. It is important not to be locked into the thinking of the past in order to express a clear vision for the future. It is equally clear that such a vision should be owned by personnel throughout the organisation as the understood driving force which energises the firm.

4. Look closely at your organisation's processes

When considering a strategic partner it is vital to be fully aware of what it is really like within your own four walls. Try to gain a knowledgeable perspective on your:

- programmes for continuing improvement and development
- policies and practices of releasing authority to encourage initiative
- generation, manipulation and usage of key information
- ability to respond to changes in the market-place.

Identify those key processes at which you are, or need to be, best. Identify those skills which you need to develop and improve. Gaining excellence in a core competence is something that requires years of consistent endeavour and application. It needs updating and renewing, but it provides probably the greatest bargaining power in negotiating a strategic partnering agreement.

Action checklist – Phase 2: Structuring the strategic partnership

5. Decide on the field of cooperation

There are three different types of strategic partnership: horizontal, vertical and diagonal.

- **Horizontal partnerships** are usually formed with former competitors from the same industry as the partnering organisation. Collaborations in research and development purposes usually come under this umbrella.
- **Vertical partnerships** are usually formed with organisations in the supply-delivery chain, such as suppliers, marketers or distributors.
- **Diagonal partnerships** are created with organisations from other industries where the focus is on deals and packages from different manufacturing sources.

In each case, complementary core competencies, strategic business fit, and ability to trust the other party are key decision areas.

6. Decide on the level of cooperation

Consider:

- which time frames are optimal for getting the project operational
- how much in terms of resources can be allocated to the project
- how formal the structure – legal form of organisation, process and communication procedures, control processes and organisation structure itself – needs to be between partners.

7. Decide on the level of involvement

To restrict the agreement to two partners may or may not be satisfactory. Strategically, innovation, production or delivery may benefit from establishing relationships with more than one partner, each bringing their own expertise and expanding the richness and the potential of the collaboration. In this case the partnership will move on from a two-way joint venture to a dynamic network of contributors. The addition of every extra partner, however, multiplies the possibility of something going wrong.

8. Decide on measurement and control issues

All strategic partnerships will need some form of control. It is vital to determine:

- which activities which partner will control
- how much control each partner will exercise
- how partners will exercise control.

It would be ideal for partners to have similar measurement systems, but this is unlikely. Contribution to, and outcomes from, the partnership may be difficult to apportion precisely when marketing and quality targets and learning objectives are key contributors to financial goals.

Action checklist – Phase 3: Selecting the partner

9. Identify intra- or extra-industry players for basic fit

This is largely a question of information gathering and analysis. Having decided on a horizontal, vertical or diagonal approach, search out the leading or emerging players which can add their strength to yours in a win-win situation. Bear in mind questions such as:

- What are the risks in such a collaboration?
- Does this potential partner have a hidden agenda?
- How turbulent is the existing/future market?
- Are there other collaborators or associates in the game?

10. Establish a partnering champion

The partnering champion should be a senior manager who commands respect at all levels, has keen powers of analysis and gets things done. The champion will be responsible for laying the framework for the partnership agreement, spreading the 'ownership' of the partnership and making it work in the start-up phase.

11. Examine strategic fit

Broad business focus is much more important than short-term goals so that the partnership fits with overall planning and does not cause a u-turn, or at least a detour. Belief systems, business plans, partnership structures and time scales will all have to follow from the business focus harmony.

12. Beware the hidden dangers

Cultural incompatibility may lurk beneath the surface of many potentially successful partnerships. Management style, organisational 'feel' and the way things really get done are difficult to quantify and all the more difficult to assimilate, and they are often impossible to impose from the outside.

Dos and don'ts for strategic partnering

Do

- Focus on business logic rather than short-term gain.
- Identify critical issues and potential obstacles.
- Build in flexible monitoring and measurement processes.

Don't

- Forget the importance of cultural fit.
- Ignore areas of potential conflict.

Further reading

BOOKS

Building strategic relationships : how to extend your organisation's reach through partnerships alliances and joint ventures, William Bergquist, Juli Betwee and David Meuel, San Francisco: Jossey Bass, 1995

Strategic partnering, Society of Management Accountants of Canada, Ontario: 1994

JOURNAL ARTICLES

Using cooperative strategies to make alliances work, Edwin R Stafford, Long Range Planning, vol 27 no 3, Jun 1994, pp64–74

Are strategic alliances working? Stratford Sherman, Fortune International, vol 126 no 6, 21 Sep 1992, pp47–48

Strategic supplier selection: understanding long-term buyer relationships, Robert E Spekman, Business Horizons, vol 31 no 4, Jul/Aug 1988, pp75–81

Developing strategic alliances: a conceptual framework for successful co-operation, Christoph Bronder and Rudolf Pritzl, European Management Journal, vol 10 no 4, Dec 1992, pp412–421

Thought starters

- What changes are affecting your markets?
- How long will such changes last?
- How swiftly can you adapt to such changes?
- Is investment in your own resource levels the best answer?

Total Quality: Mapping a TQM Strategy

This checklist provides guidance on mapping a strategy for total quality management (TQM) for those seeking to introduce TQM to the organisation for the first time. A quality strategy combines the 'hard' edge of quality (its tools and techniques) with its 'soft' side: the cultural changes you will need to achieve success. It is not just another management gimmick: it is a way of life.

The checklist is intended only as an aid to your initial thinking. Introducing TQM is a major strategic change which will require considerable research and planning. You are likely to need external advice or help to implement it.

MCI standards

This checklist has relevance for the MCI Management Standards: Key Role F – Manage Quality.

Definition

TQM is a style of managing which gives everyone in the organisation responsibility for delivering quality to the final customer, quality being described as 'fitness for purpose' or as 'delighting the customer'. TQM views each task in the organisation as fundamentally a process which is in a customer/supplier relationship with the next process. The aim at each stage is to define and meet the customer's requirements in order to maximise the satisfaction of the final consumer at the lowest possible cost.

Advantages of TQM

- It vastly improves the quality of the final product or service.
- There is a major decrease in wasted resources.
- There is a leap in productivity as staff use time more effectively.
- As products and services are improved, there should be a long-term increase in market share, leading to sustained competitive advantage.
- The workforce becomes more motivated, as employees realise their full potential.

Disadvantages of TQM

- It is extremely demanding of management and staff time.
- It can become overly bureaucratic and mechanical and lead to an emphasis on consistency rather than a focus on improvement, or the means rather than the end.
- It will only help if the organisation is heading in the right direction; it is not a tool for turning the organisation around.
- It is not a quick fix: TQM takes years to implement and is in fact an unending process.
- It can lead to too much attention being paid to the needs of final customers and not enough to those of employees.
- It is likely to cause perturbation at various stages and this has to be handled carefully.

Action checklist

1. Establish a planning team for total quality

You will need a quality team to drive through the changes. In a small organisation this will be the senior management team; in a larger one, it will comprise senior managers representing the major functions. Include in the team known sceptics or mavericks and ensure minority views are represented.

2. Assess the need to change

Consider the competitive position of the organisation. Establish who your key customers are and find out what they expect of you: don't assume that you are currently meeting all their requirements. Finding out what customers need is a continuous, not a one-off, process. Establish how other groups – suppliers, competitors and employees – view the quality of your product/service.

3. Define the vision

Draw up a vision statement defining where the organisation wants to be in terms of serving its customers: this vision must be stretching but attainable. Define the principles and values which underpin the vision. Use other organisations as a model but make sure your final draft reflects your own culture and circumstances.

4. Define the standard of service you aim to provide

Translate the vision into realistic outcomes. Establish what customers, suppliers and employees expect the organisation to deliver in quality of product/service.

5. Review how you are currently failing to meet the standards expected

There will often be a large gap between customer expectations and reality. Establish the reasons for this across the organisation. Key ones are: external constraints, being let down by suppliers and internal inefficiencies. It can happen that customers expect too little – you need to assess their needs, not only their overt wishes.

6. Conduct an organisational assessment of current levels of waste

Quantify the quality failures by securing from heads of departments an assessment of current levels of waste. Ensure they involve all employees in the assessment. Collect data as widely as possible, cost the results and present the findings to the senior management team.

7. Establish the current cost of waste

Work out how much is currently spent on rectifying internal failure (for example, reworking of below quality goods) and external failure (for example, handling customer complaints). Include appraisal costs – the time and money spent on inspection and checking.

8. Decide whether to go for third party certification

You need to decide whether to include a quality management system in your initiative. This will lead to third party certification (BS EN ISO 9000 or its equivalent), which may bring benefits with customers and suppliers or even be demanded by them.

9. Draw up your quality strategy

Use the results of the waste audit to draw up your quality strategy. This will cover:

- the goals of the strategy, including the revised mission
- the systems and tools needed to change processes
- the cultural changes needed to create the right environment for quality
- details of the resources that can be applied
- the time frames.

Secure senior management approval for the plan.

10. Draw up a management structure for change

The culture of the organisation will be critical to the success or failure of TQM. Plan for the introduction of team-based working: strong and effective teams are essential.

11. Establish an education and training programme

Some staff will need training in depth, others less so, but everyone should be given a thorough introduction to, and familiarisation with, what TQM means. Conduct an analysis of training needs in relation to TQM and cost the additional training required. This will need to be offset against the expected productivity gains. Plan for:

- general induction and training of all employees in the principles of TQM
- development of managers, supervisors and team leaders in the 'soft' skills needed to implement TQM
- job specific training in new techniques associated with TQM
- additional training in customer relations.

An external trainer or facilitator is almost always essential, especially in the early stages.

12. Opportunities and priorities for improvement

Set priorities for the introduction of TQM. Select key processes for early analysis and improvement. Do not start with more than three processes at the most. Choose at least one that is likely to demonstrate quick returns in business performance.

13. Goals and criteria for success

You will need to set both short- and long-term targets and establish measures of success both in business and cultural terms.

Useful reading

How to lead your business beyond TQM: making world class performance a reality, Michael E Joyce, London: Pitman in association with the Financial Times, 1995
Managing quality, Desmond Bell, Philip McBride and George Wilson, Oxford: Butterworth Heinemann and the Institute of Management, 1994
Beyond total quality management, Larry Reynolds, London: Sheldon Press, 1994
Understanding total quality management in a week, 2nd ed, John MacDonald, London: Hodder & Stoughton, 1998

Useful addresses

BSI Quality Assurance, 389 Chiswick High Road, London W4 4AL, Tel: 0181 996 9000
National Quality Information Centre, Institute of Quality Assurance, 10 Grosvenor Gardens, London SW1W 0DG, Tel: 0171 730 9986
Association of Quality Management Consultants, 4 Beyne Road, Olivers Battery, Winchester SO22 4JW, Tel: 01962 864394

Dos and don'ts for mapping an effective TQM strategy

Do

- Secure top management commitment from the very beginning.
- Ensure that this commitment is repeatedly conveyed.
- Involve all employees in assessing current failures.

Don't

- See TQM as a quick fix.
- Bring TQM in at the same time as several other major new initiatives.
- Use TQM (or even appear to use TQM) as a means of downsizing.

Thought starters

- Is the climate really right for the introduction of TQM? In particular, do managers have the integrity and openness which TQM will demand of them?
- Does your strategy strike the right balance between the needs of your customer and those of your employees?

Implementing Business Process Re-Engineering

This checklist provides an outline guide, as a synthesis of best practice, to the key stages in implementing Business Process Re-engineering (BPR).

BPR is multi-faceted. At its centre are two distinctive aspects: the understanding that organisations are process-driven (not function-driven); and an appreciation of the far-reaching, quantum leap approach encouraged by BPR.

BPR has many characteristics in common with Total Quality Management (TQM): both require extensive commitment from staff and rely heavily on teamwork and problem-solving to improve businesses processes in pursuit of customer satisfaction. But BPR also differs from TQM in that its essence lies in discontinuous thinking, and in rejecting the assumptions, received wisdom and routine thinking that frame the way of doing things in many businesses. In this respect it is similar to strategic benchmarking, being based on the principle that the critical review of internal processes can reveal 'break points' towards significant improvements in quality and competitiveness.

MCI standards

This checklist has relevance for the MCI Management Standards: Key Roles A and B – Manage Activities and Manage Resources.

Definition

'Re-engineering' is a way to initiate and to control change processes through imaginative analysis and systematic planning.

Any organisation (regardless of size, type or desired objective) operates fundamentally by transforming a collection of 'inputs' (for example, raw materials or raw data) into required 'outputs' (for example, products or services). This transformation involves one or more processes. In order to gain competitive advantage, an organisation must transform inputs into outputs more efficiently than its competitors by concentrating on the efficiency of these core processes. This requires regular review and improvement of the relevant processes. Hammer and Champy define BPR as:

'The fundamental rethinking and radical design of business processes to achieve dramatic improvements in critical contemporary measures of performance, such as cost, quality, service and speed.'

The improvements in process quality to be gained from BPR lie in three dimensions – process efficiency (eg cost, cycle time), product quality (eg customer satisfaction, scope and quality of product) and product development time.

Advantages of BPR

- BPR often creates new markets through the identification of 'break points'.
- BPR encourages creativity and innovation in teams.

Disadvantages of BPR

- BPR suits products and services that involve logical sequences in production. It may be less suitable for highly variable processes.
- BPR initiatives often require a high investment in IT.
- The high cost of BPR initiatives can speed up the collapse of companies already in trouble.
- BPR requires good teamwork and a high level of expertise.
- The creation of a lean organisation through 'down-sizing' may actually reduce its capacity to change.

Action checklist

1. Develop the vision – think big

Senior management needs to gain a perception of the problems in the current business. An awareness of customer expectations, competitors' advantage and opportunities resulting from IT lead this process.

Create a clear grand vision. Thinking big and bold is the essence of BPR.

2. Establish a steering committee

Membership should be cross-functional. Specialists and consultants may be included, but a balance needs to be maintained. Senior managers must lead the project and provide strategic direction. The committee needs to understand the key leverage points in the organisation. At an early stage it will need to decide whether it is going to undertake a pilot programme or go for an all-embracing project.

The committee should outline a preliminary strategy and set goals for the organisation. Use appropriate survey techniques to listen to the customer, benchmark the competition and analyse existing processes. Identify where there is a gap between performance and customer expectations.

3. Prepare the organisation for change

Communication is the key to success with change. Promote a sense of urgency. Present the business case for change, highlighting the objectives and goals of re-engineering. Encourage feedback and input from all employees.

4. Analyse existing processes

Model current processes in detail. Re-affirm which processes need to exist and why. This reduces the likelihood of past mistakes being repeated. Listen to the process owners to identify where problems exist. Document each and every helpful idea and ensure these are widely circulated. Focus the redesign on those points which can provide the greatest return.

5. Establish performance indicators or baselines

Improvements in performance can only be identified if you know where you are starting from. Performance measures include:

- transaction volumes
- cycle times
- defect rates
- customer satisfaction levels.

Make sure that the three dimensions of process efficiency, product quality and product development time are examined comprehensively. The approach adopted in strategic benchmarking can prove useful in identifying potential 'break points' for future success.

6. Redesign the process

Start with the needs of the customer and re-design the process from outside-in. Apply the following guidelines to the redesign process:

- Collect information that is required throughout the life-cycle of the process only once, at its point of origin, and make it available immediately to all who need it.
- Reduce the need for coordination by associating individuals with processes, not with departments or functions.
- Improve customer service through genuine empowerment, trust and delegation of responsibility, allowing partnerships to develop with customers and suppliers.

- Identify the key business outcomes, the business processes required to produce such outcomes and descriptions of how processes interrelate. It will also be necessary to lay out the infrastructure required to support the change by describing the:
  - management strategy, measurement systems and reward programmes
  - organisational values and individual belief systems that need to be adopted by all concerned.

7. Plan the implementation

Once a process has been redesigned an implementation plan can be prepared. Changes need time to implement, so, although BPR aims to achieve dramatic improvement in a short time, the planned schedule of change should not be unrealistically short.

Re-emphasise the need for change and communicate the vision to managers and employees to overcome the natural uncertainty that exists. Gain approval and popular support by outlining the expected benefits to be achieved by the proposed redesign.

An implementation plan should take into account that:

- schedules, budgets, completion criteria and economic justifications all need to be specified
- training will be vital to smooth the transition
- new control systems need to be established
- immediate feedback on improvements is essential
- contingencies are needed to allow for problems which will inevitably occur
- changes in physical location or layout, work flows and organisation structures, plant and IT systems, testing and pilot projects and a redefinition of roles and responsibilities will result from the process
- the plan should deliver some significant but quick results in the early stages to build commitment.

8. Monitor and evaluate progress

Monitor the process continually to ensure that the expected benefits are being obtained. Feed back results to employees to let everyone gain by knowing what has, and has not worked. This should encourage them, and also in turn help to identify further areas for improvement.

Dos and don'ts for BPR

Do

- Question all assumptions. Identify the organisation's 'sacred cows' and study them carefully.
- Choose your consultants carefully.

Don't

- Assume you are on the right BPR track merely by introducing the latest IT.
- Just settle for automating existing processes.
- Focus on individual tasks at the expense of the overall process.
- Embark on grand projects without resources and support to complete them.
- Confuse BPR with rationalisation.

Useful reading

BOOKS

Reengineering the corporation, Michael Hammer and James Champy, London: Nicholas Brealey Publishing, 1993

Business reengineering: the survival guide, Dorine C Andrews and Susan K Stalick, Eaglewood Cliffs NJ: Prentice Hall, 1994

JOURNAL ARTICLES

Reengineering work: don't automate, obliterate, Michael Hammer, Harvard Business Review, vol 90 no 4, July/August, 1990, pp104–112

Business process reengineering: evocation, elucidation and exploration, Chung For Choi and Stephen L Chan, Business Process Management Journal, vol 3 no 1, 1997, pp39–63

Reengineering. A breakthrough or little new? Sumer Aggarwal, International Journal of Technology Management, vol 13 no 3, 1997, pp326–344

Thought starters

- Do you know what proportion of resources is spent on the core processes in your organisation?
- 60% of BPR initiatives result in little or no gain – the chief causes of failure are the poor selection of consultants and inadequate commitment from the senior management team.
- If you are considering BPR, examine your reasons very carefully – they will probably indicate your probable success.

Mapping an Effective Change Programme

This checklist provides an introduction for anyone planning to implement change within the organisation. It covers any type of change programme. Its aim is to assist in the planning process by covering the basic building blocks of change.

While the pace of change may vary within organisations, there will be no remission in the extent of change in the world outside. This checklist is intended to help organisations accept change as an integral part of the management agenda, whether such change be driven by external forces such as economic or market trends, or internal forces, such as those accompanying a total quality management programme.

MCI standards

This checklist has relevance for the MCI Management Standards: Key Roles A and G – Manage Activities and Manage Projects.

Definition

The Concise Oxford Dictionary defines change as 'making or becoming different'. While this may be too vague most management dictionaries do not attempt to tackle a definition.

Managing change involves accomplishing a transition from A to B and handling the problems which arise in getting there.

Change will result as a consequence of the interaction between equipment (technology), processes (working procedures), organisation structure and people. A change to one of these four elements will inevitably lead to changes to the others, because the organisation is a living, evolving system.

Action checklist

1. Think the change through

Read a book which tackles change management; for example, John Kotter – *A Force for Change* or Rosabeth Moss Kanter – *The Change Masters*. Reading a book will take a day or two – the change process itself that you are trying to manage will take longer and cost a lot more – especially if you get it wrong.

Ask what kind of change may be involved from a broader perspective. Will it include job content, responsibility, new – unknown – tasks, new methods of working, new skills, new relationships, threats to security, new training, re-training?

Will it be something on a broader scale that involves re-thinking what the purpose of the organization is, or should be?

2. Build the change culture

Build commitment by:

- sharing information as widely as possible
- allowing for suggestions, input and differences from widespread participation
- breaking changes into manageable chunks and minimizing surprises
- making standards and requirements clear
- being honest about the downside.

Develop a culture that supports change by:

- recognizing prevalent value systems
- creating a blame-free culture of empowerment and pushing down decision-making – but clarifying decision boundaries
- breaking down departmental barriers
- designing challenging jobs
- freeing time for risk and innovation
- focusing on the interests of all stakeholders.

Get the people right by:

- recognizing staff needs and dealing with conflict positively
- being directional without being directive
- involving everyone
- earning commitment and trust
- developing relationships
- understanding how teams work
- recognizing one's limits and others' strengths.

3. Appoint a champion for change

Change programmes benefit from a 'champion' to galvanise the plan and the action. The champion's credibility is of paramount importance, as is sufficient seniority and a proven track record. The champion must also be lively, energetic, passionate and committed: if you are not the right person to be leading change, recognise it now!

4. Build the right team for change

Select a team with a mix of technical competencies and personal styles, not necessarily all at senior levels. Most members should be respected individuals from within the organisation, not outsiders. You need 'movers and shakers' whose commitment is not in doubt, but temper them with a few known cynics. All should have earned respect within the organisation and be widely trusted and credible.

5. Build the case for change

Develop an outline of what the organisation will look like at the end of the culture change programme. Include structures and culture: will you move from a hierarchical to a team-based culture? What will the implications be?

You might know why the organisation needs to change but you need to persuade others; everyone must be convinced of the urgency of the need. Draw up a clear, compelling case which marshals both quantitative and qualitative arguments. Spell these out in terms of business objectives linked to a vision of where the organisation will be if change is successful.

In reality, persuading people of the need for change can be a complex and sensitive business which can appear odd if it comes 'out of the blue'. It may be useful to bring someone in from the outside to act as a catalyst but this needs to be managed with care and sensitivity.

Given that the changes are best owned by the people implementing them, it is most practical to get a group of staff to identify the change factors themselves – then they see and understand the need for change.

A health-check of the key factors in mapping change includes:

- **Leadership** – Does the leader set an example and foster learning and development?
- **People** – Do people think naturally about what's coming next? Or will the next change be met with the same old shock and horror?
- **Control** – Do measurement and procedural control stifle creativity?
- **Integration** – Do we have a business of people in separate boxes or do we mix across areas and responsibilities?
- **Processes** – Which are the key activities which give us our strength?

6. Define the scope of change

To be successful, a change programme must have the right scope. Define its coverage and limits rigorously. To be fully effective change needs to operate in six dimensions:

- markets and customers
- products and services

- business processes
- people and reward systems
- structure and facilities
- technologies.

7. Draw up an outline plan

Plan for change in the way you would for any major project. Cover:

- Vision: what is the 'big idea' behind the change? What is the organisation striving to achieve? This must be clear and compelling.
- Scope: what needs to change if the organisation is to realise its vision?
- Time frame: what will change when, and in what order? Radical change takes time, especially if attitude change is involved.
- People: who will be most affected by change and how? Who will play prominent roles in implementing change (the change agents)?
- Resources: how much will the change cost? Will there be offsetting benefits?
- Communications: will you need new mechanisms and structures to communicate with front line employees?
- Training: have you allowed for the training of managers and front line employees in both hard and soft skills associated with change?
- Organisation structure: will changes be needed, for example towards a flatter structure?

8. Cost the change programme

Change can be expensive, particularly if it is associated with plant closure or redundancies. Recognise this and draw up a separate budget. Don't underestimate the 'softer' costs of training, or the communications the programme will require.

9. Analyse your management competencies

Senior managers need to be fully committed to change programmes to guarantee their success. Establish from the outset whether the management team is signed up to change, and address honestly the position of those who are not enthusiastic supporters. Make sure that senior managers are included in those consulted for proposing change factors.

10. Identify the driving and restraining forces

In any organisation, there will be forces driving and forces restraining change: you need to identify both sets. Plan to reinforce the drivers, or add new ones; and to weaken or lessen the restraining forces, through education. This will usually be a slow process, but it can be helped by frank discussion, and even more by positive success.

11. Outline the change programme to line managers

Use your plan to outline to line managers the likely impact of the programme on structures, people, processes and products. Seek criticism and feedback and use them to refine the plan and build consensus in favour of change.

12. Communicate

Communication is the key to successful change. Communicate continuously with stakeholders – employees, customers, suppliers and owners – as you plan and build the programme. Be open and honest with employees about the likely extent of change. Don't allow rumour to circulate: be frank.

13. Identify change agents

Although change is initiated at the top, and led by a change team, it has to be driven through the organisation by change agents. These need to be the organisation's own employees, not external consultants. Select people who are committed, enthusiastic and who can command respect. Plan to train them and use them to champion and cascade the change programme throughout the organisation.

Dos and don'ts for effective change

Do

- Think big: many change programmes fail to deliver the expected results because their ambitions are too narrow, or not radical enough.
- Tap diversity: find out the opinions of newcomers and 'outsiders' within the organisation and tap the views of customers and suppliers.
- Be patient and persistent: change takes time.

Don't

- Underestimate the cost of change: build in costings for repeated communications and training efforts.
- Embark on a major change programme until you are convinced you have the absolute support of the top management team.
- Bulldoze through resisters to change; instead listen and persuade.

Useful reading

How to be better at managing change, D E Hussey, London: Kogan Page, 1998

Create that change: readymade tools for change management, Steve Smith, ed., London: Kogan Page, 1997

A real life guide to organizational change, George Blair and Sandy Meadows, Aldershot: Gower, 1996

Thought starters

- Is an assessment of what the customer wants at the heart of your change strategy?
- Do you have relevant measures to indicate your efficiency and effectiveness?
- Do you have a realistic assessment of staff morale?

Implementing an Effective Change Programme

This checklist is intended for those who have mapped a change pro-gramme for the organisation (See the previous checklist for details on Mapping an Effective Change Programme] and are now ready to imple-ment it. It provides pointers to the issues you will need to consider in bringing in change, rather than providing a detailed implementation schedule: this will vary according to the organisation and the nature of the change.

MCI standards

This checklist has relevance for the MCI Management Standards: Key Roles A and G – Manage Activities and Manage Projects.

Definition

This checklist covers any type of major change programme within an organi-sation. These range from those driven by external forces – changes in the market; in customer demands; in legislation or regulation – to those which are internally driven, for example, to accompany a total quality management programme.

Change will result as a consequence of the interaction between equipment (technology), processes (working procedures), organisation structure and people; a change to one of these four elements will inevitably cause changes to the others, because the organisation is a living, evolving system.

Managing change involves accomplishing a transition from A to B and han-dling the problems which arise in getting there.

Action checklist

1. Agree the implementation strategy

The details of the strategy need to be clear before you begin to embark on change. Is implementation going to be top-down or bottom-up or a mix of both? Will the change be made by division, by department or in a 'big bang' approach?

2. Agree the time frame

Every change programme needs a start date and a finite time span, regardless of whether it is being introduced incrementally or simultaneously across divisions. The time table must be stretching enough to convey urgency but attainable enough to be motivating.

3. Draw up detailed implementation plans

Combine the strategy and timetable to draw up detailed implementation plans with each divisional or departmental head. Use the change team as a source of advice and consultancy, but empower line managers to determine how they will implement the details of change against the overall goals.

The change programme is unlikely to be the only corporate initiative underway. Ensure the strategy and goals behind the others are consistent and point in the same direction. Do employees receive consistent messages about the organisation's core values and beliefs from each of the programmes?

4. Set up a team of stakeholders

This does not include top management but will benefit from top management sponsorship. The team will include the key people involved in designing and delivering the service as well as those receiving it. They will also be responsible for defining and disseminating the benefits of the change.

5. Establish good project management

Treat change like any project. Set goals and milestones and monitor progress to keep the project on schedule and on budget. Flag up potential problems as early as possible and plan for them with contingencies. Establish the project team ground-rules especially on information sharing, decision-making and reporting.

6. Personalise the case for change

People will only take on board the case for change when they can personalise it and relate it to their own job and team. Ensure that your line managers translate the corporate case for change into reality for every individual in the company. Consider what change will mean for each individual in terms of: status (job title, budget responsibility); habits (changes to working time, new colleagues); beliefs (move to a customer focus); and behaviour (new working practices).

7. Ensure participation

Individual employees must feel they can take ownership of the change programme as it evolves. Change can be stressful if imposed. Introduce mechanisms to facilitate this. Allow criticism and feedback but ensure the means exist to take corrective action.

8. Create a sense of purpose and urgency to tackle real problems, which have prevented progress in the past

Ask what and who is preventing progress and who can really help in unblocking it.

Think of breaking the code of silence that engenders organisational protectionism and maintains the status quo.

9. Motivate

Sustained change requires very high levels of motivation. People need to feel valued, to be developed, to have their achievements recognised, and to be challenged. Recognise that different rewards will motivate different people to change.

10. Be prepared for conflict

Change usually brings about conflict of one kind or another, simply because people have different views and reactions. Try to get conflict to surface rather than fester; try to tackle it by dissecting and analysing it with those who are experiencing it. Often enough conflict can be put to positive work through open discussion and clarification.

11. Be willing to negotiate

When conflict cannot be resolved through improved explanation and discussion, you will have to negotiate and persuade. This means avoiding entrenched positions, and working out how to shift others from theirs. It means getting to an agreed 'yes' without either side winning or losing face.

12. Anticipate stress

It is uncertainty rather than change that really worries employees. Provide as much information as possible and quash rumours as soon as they arise.

Any change programme is stressful. Fear of the unknown rather than change itself is the major contributory factor. Reduce its impact by being as open as possible about all the consequences of change. See that employees own the changes.

13. Build skills

View the change programme as a learning process and integrate it into the corporate training programme. Build both technical and soft skills at all levels within the organisation. Set an example by updating the skills of top management.

14. Build in capability for learning

Creating goals and plans that everyone subscribes to means that everyone can gain. Turn learning into something that people want to buy into – instead of it being perceived as a chore – where they can feel the 'buzz' of discovery and involvement in new developments.

15. Remember change is discontinuous

Change is a very long process made up of very small and often invisible modifications to behaviour and attitudes. Seek innovative ways to remind staff of the overall case for change and to reinforce its value to them.

Accept that change will be a stop/start process. Plan for this and develop strategies to gear the organisation up for renewed effort if there are setbacks.

16. Monitor and evaluate

Monitor and evaluate the results of the change programme against the goals and milestones established in the original plan. Are these goals still appropriate or do they need to be revised in the light of experience?

Existing performance measures may transmit the wrong signals and act as a block on change. Design measures which are consistent with the vision and goals.

Be honest in your assessment of progress. If there is a real divergence between the plan goals and reality take corrective action quickly. Be open about failure and involve employees in setting new targets or devising new measures.

Dos and don'ts for effective change

Do
- Plan to deliver early tangible results and publicise successes to build momentum and support.
- Select priorities for change rather than attempt to address everything at once.
- Involve employees at every stage of designing and implementing change.
- Make sure you have top management sponsorship of and commitment to the agreed implementation.

Don't
- Fail to appreciate the depth of resistance there may be to change. Plan for resistance and cost it in terms of additional training and communications.
- Get lost in detail or lose sight of the vision: real change often comes through a simple breakthrough.
- Skimp on the resources for training or communications.

Useful reading

How to be better at managing change, D E Hussey, London: Kogan Page, 1998

Create that change: readymade tools for change management, Steve Smith, ed., London: Kogan Page, 1997

A real life guide to organizational change, George Blair and Sandy Meadows, Aldershot: Gower, 1996

Better change: best practices for transforming your organisation, Price Waterhouse Change Integration Team, New York: Irwin Professional Publishing, 1995

A manual for change, Terry Wilson, Aldershot: Gower, 1994

A force for change: how leadership differs from management, John P Kotter, New York: Free Press, 1990

The change masters: corporate entrepreneurs at work, Rosabeth Moss Kanter, London: Unwin Paperbacks, 1988

Thought starters

- Which indicators will tell you if change has really been effected?
- What signals should top management send to employees to show the extent of their commitment to change?
- What messages will indicate successful staff ownership of change?

Developing a Strategy for World Class Business

This checklist provides an introductory framework for managers whose companies wish to pursue the route to world class status. The responsibility for a world class strategy usually rests with the chief executive and senior management.

Becoming a world class company is not a simple process, and requires effort and commitment from the entire organisation. Developing a strategy for action is essential if world class status is to be achieved.

MCI standards

This checklist has relevance for the MCI Management Standards: Key Role A – Manage Activities.

Definition

'World class' is a concept that is difficult to define. However, an accepted working definition is that a world class company should be able to compete with any other organisation in its chosen markets and that it aspires to world-beating standards in everything it does, in every department or division. 'World class' also embraces the practice of (and excellence in) techniques such as total quality management, continuous improvement, customer service, international benchmarking, flexible working and training. 'World class' organisations also accept the necessity for continuous change.

Action checklist

1. Consider outside influences

Identify the factors in the external environment which call for a strategic response from your business. These can be grouped under main headings such as: economic factors; demographic trends; environmental factors; technology; suppliers and competition.

2. Establish the world class vision

Determine the core business of your organisation – that at which your organisation should excel. Top management must make a vision of excellence clear in a brief statement which is impossible to misinterpret. In addition to helping form this vision, the chief executive's role is to clarify the message, push forward change, and champion the ideas and capabilities which will beat your competitors.

3. Analyse your current position

Benchmark your organisation against your competitors as far as you can. This can be very difficult, as much of the necessary information may not be available. However, organisations do exist to help in this process (see Useful addresses).

Consider the following areas:

- your product
- its price
- its availability
- your customer service
- your policy for continuous improvement
- your costs
- your market share.

Do you match your competitors in these areas, or is your organisation well below or considerably better than them? Don't limit this measure to competitors in your own country – compare yourself against world wide competition. Identify which organisations are excellent within these areas and determine what makes them the best (in order to beat them!).

Additionally, assess where you stand in customers' eyes. What is their perception of your status compared to your competitors?

4. Focus on core capabilities

From the analyses of the external environment, the core business of the organisation, and the standing of competitors, draw up a list of the core capabilities of your organisation which will enable you to compete in world markets. Core capabilities will include:

- product knowledge / service skills
- marketing skills
- innovation / research capacity
- financial planning and control
- human resource capabilities (including motivation as well as skills).

Determine which of these core capabilities need extra focus, and resource their development.

5. Build a corporate strategy

Focus on achieving better products or services, better factories or service operations, better organisation, better management, and better information and communication.

Ask yourself questions such as:

- Have the key business processes been defined and understood?
- Has a quality, or customer focus ethic been established throughout the organisation?
- Are quality and reliability of products and services measured?
- Are the key performance measures improving / reviewed?
- Is everyone in the organisation informed of results and developments?
- Is customer satisfaction monitored on a regular basis?
- Are employees multi-skilled? Are they flexible and willing to adapt?
- Do your employees have continuing personal development plans in place?
- How are creativity and innovation encouraged and nurtured?
- How well does communication flow?
- Does it flow in all directions?

6. Set high targets for the organisation

Set imaginative and ambitious targets by identifying where you intend to be in one, three and five years' time. If targets are easily achievable there is a danger that you will rest on your laurels. Being satisfied with these improvements means never becoming world class.

- Ensure that organisational targets are translated into divisional and departmental goals which are incorporated into individual objectives.
- Get staff into the habit of setting their own targets (they will usually be higher than those you would set them).

7. Develop simple performance measures

Measurement processes – as simple and straightforward as possible – allow you to continuously monitor what is happening, and continuously report on progress. Performance measures must be relevant to your aims – concentrate on customer service, time reduction and quality – and remember that within a world class company, financial measures are not the most important performance measure in terms of achieving your objectives.

8. Adopt straightforward reporting procedures

Complex reports are time-consuming to understand, require a lot of preparation and consequently tend to be produced monthly at best. World class companies must be able to act immediately on the results of performance measurement; if a report takes three weeks to generate, then this three week lead-time will impact on continuous improvement. Adopt the one-page management reporting rule.

9. Communicate your progress

Nothing inspires and motivates like success itself. Your employees must be kept fully informed of the organisation's progress (get your staff to produce their own progress charts if possible). By adopting simple measurement techniques, results can be given to employees on a daily basis via bulletin or notice boards – preferably in a graphic or pictorial form. Progress reports can be an inspirational form of communication: poor communication is a reason why many things go wrong.

10. Revise your performance targets

As your organisation raises its performance in the areas you have defined, identify new areas to be improved. As areas improve, their reports should reduce to exception reporting (a report showing only those items which deviate from plan or the established norm), allowing the organisation to focus on new needs.

How to assess effectiveness

Becoming world class, although an achievement, is not the end of the process. To be a world class company you must continue to benchmark yourself against your competitors regularly. If you fail to do this, your organisation will slip from the position it has achieved to be replaced by another – staying world class is just as hard as becoming world class, if not harder.

Dos and don'ts for world class firms

Do
- Continue to set challenging targets for your organisation.
- Use flexibility and adaptability – but within limits.
- Have a bias towards action and controlled risk.
- Focus on continuous improvement.
- Keep a close and continuous eye on major competitors.
- Be sensitive to the conditions, context and methods of local cultures.

Don't
- Become complacent once you feel you are world class.
- Belittle the importance of measures and reports.
- Attempt to impose 'accepted' corporate ways and means across borders.

Useful reading

BOOKS

World class manufacturing management directions, Nick Parker and Ray Irving, Corby: Institute of Management Foundation, 1996

World class manufacturing: the next decade, Richard J Schonberger, New York: Simon and Schuster, 1996

World class manufacturing, Jim Todd, London: McGraw Hill, 1994

JOURNAL ARTICLES

Measuring performance against world class standards, Ron Basu and Nevan Wright, IIE Solutions, December 1996, pp32–35

World class competitiveness, Steve Smith, Managing Service Quality, vol 5 no 5, 1995, pp36–42

From ugly ducklings to elegant swans: transforming parochial firms into world leaders, Constantinos Markides and John M Stopford, Business Strategy Review, vol 6 no 2, 1995, pp1–24

Useful addresses

Benchmarking Centre, Truscon House, Station Road, Gerrards Cross, Bucks, Tel: 01753 890070

Benchmarking Council, PIMS Associates, 15 Basing Hall Street, London EC2V 5BR, Tel: 0171 776 2800

Centre for Interfirm Comparison, Capital House, 48 Andover Road, Winchester, Hants SO23 7BH, Tel: 01962 844144

The Institute of Management, Management House, Cottingham Road, Corby, Northants NN17 1TT, Tel: 01536 204222

Thought starters

- Do you know the key performers in your industry?
- What approaches to ensuring and measuring customer satisfaction do you have in place?
- Do you have the means of measuring the quality of your organisation's performance?
- Do you set high targets which are measured, reviewed and renewed?

Developing a Manufacturing Strategy

This checklist has been designed to explain the basic steps in analysing existing manufacturing activities and reviewing current manufacturing strategy.

Most organisations operate with a business plan and a broad corporate strategy, but not all manufacturing companies have a manufacturing strategy, and many of those that do, fail to update it on a regular basis. Competitive advantage can be gained by having a superior mix of people, technology, focus and direction. A manufacturing strategy explores all these issues. The time scale of completing a radical manufacturing change dictates that a long-term view is essential to permit planned investment and implementation.

MCI standards

This checklist has relevance for the MCI Management Standards: Key Roles A and B – Manage Activities and Manage Resources.

Definition

A manufacturing strategy is a working document which outlines:

- the basis for competitive advantage
- the key issues which will affect the organisation
- the strategic manufacturing aims
- the broad strategic initiatives to be pursued.

The latter should cover quality, technology, skill requirements, training and make-or-buy decisions.

Action checklist

1. Appoint a project team

The planning of a strategy requires the full-time attention of a number of knowledgeable people from the management team. Team members need to have a detailed understanding of the aims of the organisation, its products

and markets, and manufacturing technology. Skills in competitor analysis
are also useful.

2. Gain an understanding of the existing market position

A thorough understanding of your existing products is essential to the strategy formulation process. Ask:

- by what strategy does your organisation compete? The three generic
  strategies are competing on cost (cost leadership), on superior features or
  service (differentiation), or on a subset of the market (niche market
  focus).
- what product families do you have? Use product life cycles as a framework
  for thinking about the manufacturing requirements of different products.
  Plotting product life cycles for existing key products and future projects can
  build a picture of the size and shape of the business in the future.

In addition:

- measure the performance of each product. Focus upon the contribution,
  market share, and market growth.
- identify the competitive edge produced by each product family.
  Competitive features might include quality, delivery lead time, delivery
  flexibility, design flexibility or price. Determine the criteria which give
  you the greatest competitive advantage.

3. Identify the drivers of change

Consider:

- business criteria (product performance, market demands, the evolution of
  manufacturing philosophies and management structures)
- technological developments
- financial pressures.

Analyse external influences on the organisation, internal resources and capabilities, and the skills and competencies of staff by undertaking a SWOT
analysis.

4. Analyse your current performance

Assessing your performance against competitive edge criteria can be difficult.
Some factors are not easy to measure directly, while comparative data may
be hard to obtain. Use techniques such as Pareto analysis and activity sam-
pling to facilitate data collection. Focus upon product performance features,
such as quality, delivery, flexibility, material costs and capital costs. Obtain
comparative data through published reports, databases, or by talking to customers and suppliers. Consider destructive analysis of a competitor's
product. Participate in benchmarking studies.

5. Identify critical components

The identification of those components most critical to the long-term success of the organisation helps you to maximise the use of the limited investment capital available. Components can be placed on a continuum of high or low business content, with those at the high end being of strategic importance. Components with a high added value should be added to the list of strategic components whilst those with a low business content should be considered for buying-in.

- Identify the major part families and describe their manufacturing characteristics.
- List the key facilities needed to manufacture the strategic components.

6. Assess your manufacturing operation

This can be a complicated task, so give yourself plenty of time.

Examine current practice with regard to a range of criteria. The nine key areas most often covered include facilities, span of process (the degree of vertical integration), capacity, processes and the way they are organised, human resources, quality, control policies, suppliers and new products.

Compare the strengths and weaknesses of current practice with your established competitive edge criteria. Where are the gaps?

7. Set new targets

Without tough targets it is difficult not only to measure achievement, but to maintain the necessary top-down pressure to achieve them. Targets can be wide-ranging and cover such criteria as tooling costs, the utilisation of equipment, defective materials or inventory.

8. Develop a new manufacturing strategy

You are now ready to compile your new manufacturing strategy.

Using your knowledge of your most important product families, your competitive advantage criteria, and the existing performance gaps, identify the weaknesses of the existing policies. Discuss possible actions and strategic choices. Consider running a simulation to test these options.

9. Develop your supplier network

For those components which you have decided to buy in, you should go through the process of identifying a potential supplier network and evaluating its ability to meet the demands of in-house manufacture. Consider your relationship with each supplier.

As with all business plans, review your manufacturing plan annually against the developing business situation and set revised targets.

Useful reading

Strategic manufacturing for competitive advantage: transforming operations from shop floor to strategy, Steve Brown, Hemel Hempstead: Prentice Hall, 1996

Competitive manufacturing: a practical approach to the development of a manufacturing strategy, Rev ed, Department of Trade and Industry, Bedford: IFS International, 1994

Manufacturing strategy: the strategic management of the manufacturing function, 2nd ed, Terry Hill, London: MacMillan, 1993

Manufacturing strategy: formulation and implementation, Garry Robert Greenhalgh, Wokingham: Addison-Wesley, 1991

Useful address

Institute of Operations Management, University of Warwick Science Park, Sir William Lyons Road, Coventry CV4 7EZ, Tel: 01203 692266

Dos and don'ts for developing a manufacturing strategy

Do

- Have a thorough understanding of your existing manufacturing strategy.
- Ensure you know the strengths and weaknesses of your existing product line.

Don't

- Finish your strategy and leave it on the shelf – it should be revised to meet changing market conditions.

Thought starters

- Do you have a manufacturing strategy?
- Is it reviewed on a regular basis?
- What are the strengths, weaknesses, opportunities and threats to your existing product line?

Moving towards the Virtual Organisation

This checklist is written for those managers wishing to know the major philosophies underlying the term 'the virtual organisation' and the key factors involved in it.

The concept of the virtual organisation embraces changes to established organisational structures and methods of working, many of which are happening today, and others which may seem futuristic to us. This checklist does not advocate revolutionary change but describes the considerations involved in an evolutionary approach towards the virtual organisation. Some kinds of organisation will find it easier to embrace virtuality than others, but all managers need to familiarise themselves with what has been described as the management model of tomorrow.

MCI standards

This checklist has relevance for the MCI Management Standards: Key Roles A and B – Manage Activities and Manage Resources.

Definition

There is no single definition of the virtual organisation. Most writers agree, however, that it embraces the concept of organisational flexibility unconstrained by the traditional barriers of place and time. Essentially it relies on the exploitation of cyberspace – the electronic medium for data exchange brought about by the integration of telecommunications and computer software. It indicates notions of a hidden reality behind the scenes, where results are not achieved in traditional ways. It describes the thought that an organisation, team, individual, service, or even product need not be 'physically there' although they appear so; real but not real. It is a term which brings together the various initiatives which organisations are exploring to make themselves more responsive to changes in today's marketplace.

Benefits of virtuality

- Distance is no object to the accomplishment of work, meetings, collaborations or conferences.
- Significant productivity improvements.
- Reduction of overhead costs.
- Work can be spread across time zones.
- Organisations can focus on what they are best at.

Requirements for virtuality

The benefits of the virtual organisation cannot be realised unless:

- staff are empowered and trusted
- a reciprocal loyalty is established between employee and employer
- all employees, not just knowledge workers, are involved
- management is prepared to question the older, accepted methodologies and to explore new ways of working.

Action checklist: Becoming aware

1. Take account of the changing marketplace

Assess what your organisation is doing strategically to respond to change, remain competitive and meet the demands of customers. How will you:

- penetrate new markets and cut costs?
- meet ever-higher levels of quality and still increase speed-to-market?

2. Think about where you want to be in the future

Thinking of your organisation's future means analysing where you are now and how you got there, and determining where you want to be in the future and planning how you are going to get there. This involves working out what your organisation is best at and knowing how to successfully deploy its skills and resources.

Adopt a clear vision for the future which provides both a destination and framework for planning, objective-setting, decision making and action.

3. Beware of continual downsizing

Try to analyse where downsizing is taking you; slimmer may not mean fitter. Fitter means considering new ways of working, not just reducing numbers and leaving others to fill the gaps. Downsizing should be the result of a reengineering effort which leads you to greater efficiencies after due analysis of work processes, and the capability of available technology.

4. Beware of fixed structures

Fixed, hierarchical structures have been slow to respond to a fast-changing market. Think instead of flexible structures which make exploitation of opportunities easier by allowing organisations to pull together resources from both inside and outside the organisation according to need.

Action checklist: Taking steps

1. Take advantage of the communications revolution

Barriers to the adoption of IT by businesses are being overcome due to cheaper, ever more powerful hardware and software and wider computer literacy. The convergence of IT with telecommunications has seen an explosion in data-sharing between individuals who are physically remote from each other. Start taking advantage of this revolution by:

- using e-mail as a cheap alternative to letters, fax or phone
- exploring Computer Telephony Integration (CTI), which allows a caller to be identified and their record to appear on the computer screen before, or as, the operator answers the phone
- buying laptop computers so that employees can be more mobile. With a laptop anyone can take their office anywhere at any time.

2. Consider the new ways of working

Look at the various options which give both the employer and employee flexibility in where and how work is done. These options include:

- **electronic mail (e-mail)** – allows people to work together even if they are not in the same room or building
- **groupware** – permits interactive dialogues on-screen between many people simultaneously whilst accessing the same corporate information
- **video-conferencing** – live audio and video connections link people in remote locations
- **teleworking** – a homeworker connected to work through telecommunications equipment
- **hot-desking** – where an employee does not have their own desk but is allocated one on arrival in the building
- **hotelling** – where clients provide a desk.

Consideration of such options must involve a willingness to cast off old assumptions and values, such as the need to bring the worker to the office, that employees who work unseen are not to be trusted, and that distance is a barrier to communication.

Also compare the cost benefits. The added costs of computing and telecommunications equipment may be insignificant when compared with the potential savings on overhead costs, such as office space and travel.

3. Consider outsourcing to enhance your competitiveness

Analysing your organisation's core competencies will help you to identify support activities for outsourcing; you may have already started with cleaning and catering services and may move on to training and IT. Before you do this, consider the problems raised by outsourcing as well as the benefits.

4. Find collaborative partners and alliances

Virtual organisations may extend beyond the boundary of any one formal organisation in two different ways:

- strategic partnerships and alliances
- a temporary network of independent companies where resources, skills and costs are shared to exploit market opportunities.

Finding the right partner may not be as easy as it seems; considerations include:

- the right fit of competencies
- shared values
- mutual trust to stand alongside formal structures and agreements
- the division of responsibility for marketing strategies
- the sharing of finance for the project.

5. Build information systems that work for your customers

Database systems can be exploited to do more than merely store, handle, sort and retrieve information. They can be integrated with other systems such as CTI or the Internet, to provide enhanced customer service. The important factor is to know what is technically possible, what you want to achieve and to build a system to provide what customers need. Delivering a first-class customer service no longer relies on you being in the office; instead it can be provided through IT.

6. Manage the human implications

Think about the human reaction to change: employees appreciate the social aspects of work (which can be threatened by virtual working); managers fear a lack of control of people who they cannot see. A shift in attitudes is demanded on the part of both organisations and individuals.

Such changes cannot happen overnight, however. Identify other organisations which are using virtuality and see what you can learn from their experience.

Dos and don'ts associated with moving towards the virtual organisation

Do

- Ask yourself where the organisation will be in 5 years' time.
- Look at what competitors are doing.
- Remember it's an evolutionary process.
- Weigh up the cost implications of IT/communications technologies.
- Think in terms of genuine trust between colleagues, staff and partners.

Don't

- Ignore how IT and telecommunications can change the way you do business.
- Underestimate the pitfalls in changing traditional ways of working.
- Think in terms of fixed structures.

Useful reading

BOOKS

Agile competitors and virtual organizations: strategies for enriching the customer, Steven L Goldman, Roger N Nagel, and Kenneth Preiss, New York: Van Nostrand Reinhold, 1995
Creating tomorrow's organization: unlocking the benefits of future work, David Birchall and Laurence Lyons, London: Pitman, 1995
The virtual corporation: structuring and revitalizing the corporation for the 21st century, William H Davidow and Michael S Malone, New York: Harper Collins, 1992

JOURNAL ARTICLES

The virtual corporation: the company of the future will be the ultimate in adaptability, John A Byrne, Richard Brandt and Otis Port, International Business Week, No 3292, 8 February 1993, pp36–41
Office space, cyberspace and virtual organization, Christopher Barnatt, Journal of General Management, Vol 20 no 4, Summer 1995, pp78–91
Trust and the virtual organization, Charles Handy, Harvard Business Review, Vol 73 no 3, May/June 1995, pp40–42,44, 46–50
The core competencies of the corporation, C K Prahalad and G Hamel, Harvard Business Review, Vol 68 no 3, May/June 1990, pp79–91

Thought starters

- 'How do you manage people whom you do not see?' (Handy)
- 'In the future, some organizational functions may exist solely in computer systems' (Barnatt)

Deciding Whether to Outsource

This checklist is for those who must address the decision of whether to outsource or not, and if so, what and how to outsource. The checklist encompasses the stages in the outsourcing process leading up to drawing up and testing a contract.

Seen usually as a threat by employees and an opportunity by organisations, outsourcing is rapidly becoming more accepted. In addition to the inevitable driver of cost-savings, there are many contributory elements which lead an organisation to consider outsourcing, in particular the need for flexibility as demand for products or services rises and falls, and ways of delivering them improve.

On the surface the benefits of outsourcing seem not only straightforward but also considerable. Experience shows, however, that there are many pitfalls, dangers and costs.

MCI standards

This checklist has relevance for the MCI Management Standards: Key Roles B and C – Manage Resources and Manage People.

Definition

Increasingly, outsourcing is understood to mean the retention of responsibility for services by the organisation but devolution of the day-to-day performance of those services to an external organisation, usually under a contract with agreed standards, costs and conditions.

In this checklist the organisation considering outsourcing some or part of its functions will be called the Organisation; the external organisation to take them on will be called the Agency.

Advantages of outsourcing

For the Organisation the decision to outsource takes place for reasons of:

- cost and efficiency savings
- greater financial flexibility through reduced overheads
- operational flexibility and control through contractual relationships
- a wish or a need to focus on core activities
- access to better management skills on non-core activities
- staffing flexibility.

Disadvantages of outsourcing

- Changing support functions may bring about reduced robustness.
- Information flows with the Agency will need careful coordination.
- Reduced learning capacity through a depleted skill-base.
- Declining morale and motivation as jobs appear to 'go'.
- Reduced ability to integrate processes.
- Possible lack of control over activities outsourced.
- Increased insecurity, whether staff remain in the Organisation, or are taken on by the Agency.

Action checklist

1. Establish the outsourcing project team

Treat the outsourcing proposal like a project. Apply the principles of project management, especially selecting a project leader and team, establishing terms of reference, a method of working and an action plan.

2. Analyse your current position

Ideally, you should have carried out a radical review of the organisation's processes – you don't want to outsource an activity that might be better integrated with another you regard as 'core'. Ensure you have assessed:

- the advantage to be achieved by concentration on core services
- minimum involvement required in things that don't affect the customer
- control required of non-diminishing, non-productive overheads
- functions which are more viable through an external agency
- a clear vision of where the business is to be.

3. Pay attention to people

As the contract stage approaches, people will suffer from anxiety and uncertainty. At best their working life will transfer from one employer to another, at worst their job could be lost. Keep people at the forefront of your thinking.

4. Benchmark

Someone, somewhere is probably doing the same thing in a better way, or in the same way at lower cost. Identify appropriate organisations to benchmark against and establish which activities they are outsourcing.

5. Come to a decision

Decide which are your core areas – Tom Peters said: '...do what you do best and outsource the rest'. The principal questions are:

- what is core to the business and to the future of the business?
- what can bring competitive advantage?

Then, decide whether outsourcing should become policy for organisation-wide application to non-core areas or if it is to be used as the need arises.

6. Decide what to outsource

Logically, what to outsource follows from the decision process. If you focus on the core competencies of your organisation, on your uniqueness, then targets for outsourcing become those areas which make up the support, administration, routine and internal servicing of the organisation.

Areas which have traditionally been subject to outsourcing include legal services, transport, catering, printing, advertising, accounting, and, especially, auditing and security. More recently these have been joined by data processing, IT services, information processing, public relations, buildings management and training.

Staff are usually transferred with the function to the Agency. Obviously, this is an area which requires great consideration and sensitivity.

7. Tender the package

The tender is both an objective document detailing the services, activities and targets required, and a selling document which serves to attract those Agencies which can add to the Organisation's capability. Outsourcing is not just a matter of getting rid of problem areas.

Once an attractive package has been defined, send an outline specification and request for information to those Agencies likely to be interested. The outline specification contains the broad intention of the outsourcing proposal and the time-scales the Organisation has in mind. The request for information is a questionnaire-type eligibility test intended to establish the level of the Agency's competence and interest. The second stage is the invitation to tender – a precise document which spells out exactly what Agencies are required to bid for.

8. Choose a partner

The tender process should be used for the evaluation of facts, but choosing an outsourcing partner is much more than choosing a new supplier, because the process involves a customised service, agreement on service levels and a contract. At this stage the Organisation will be looking for an Agency with which it can share objectives and values, have regular senior management meetings, and disclose otherwise confidential information. Harmony of management styles is a key requisite for success. The Organisation will also look for:

- evidence of quality management
- a proven track record, a flexible approach and financial viability
- experience in handling the sensitive issue of staff absorption
- how important in turnover the contract is for the Agency.

9. Meet the staff

It is essential that the Agency meets its prospective new staff before any contracts are signed. Allowing concerns to be aired and questions to be asked may help to reduce feelings of being 'dumped' or cast aside. On the other hand, glaring conflicts in style and personalities may emerge which can have an important impact on the contractual stage. Many other issues involving terms and conditions of employment will need addressing, including those of appropriate compensation if Agency employment is not available or not required.

10. Draw up the contract

If it is to be the project team that draws up the contract it will need to have a strong legal input, especially on TUPE – the Transfer of Undertakings (Protection of Employment) Regulations 1981. Contained within the contract should be:

- minimum service levels that the Agency will provide, and checks and controls that these are met – perhaps via a liaison manager – and clauses including remedies or financial compensation if they are not
- demarcation of service responsibilities and boundaries so that both Organisation and Agency are clear on who is doing what
- who owns what in terms of equipment and hardware
- the fate of the staff to be outsourced and details of their terms and conditions of employment
- flexibility and allowance for change, for example if business volumes double or halve

- a contract term, with a review date and provision for the outsourced function to revert to the Organisation
- a 'what-if' honeymoon period before the contract becomes fully enforced.

11. Test the contract

Ensure that the contract will stand up to the rigours and complexities of the operation in action. A period of testing and trial is ideal for making adjustments before the contract becomes final and to examine the possibility of the partnership breaking down.

Dos and don'ts of outsourcing

Do

- Outsource the 'doing' of an activity, not the responsibility for it.
- Understand the scope of the services to be outsourced.
- Have a clear vision of what outsourcing should achieve.

Don't

- Let the goal of cost savings dominate everything else.
- Think that outsourcing is the answer to all problems.
- Outsource strategic, customer or financial management.

Useful reading

BOOK

The truth about outsourcing, Brian Rothery and Ian Robertson, Aldershot: Gower, 1995

JOURNAL ARTICLES

Do the right thing, John Bell, Business and Technology Magazine, April 1995, pp50–51
Culture, community and networks: the hidden costs of outsourcing, John Hendry, European Management Journal, Vol 13 no 2, June 1995, pp193–200
Outsourcing: making the decision, Malcolm Wheatley, Human Resources UK, January/February 1995, no 16, pp63–64, 66, 68

Useful Organisations

British Institute of Facilities Management, 67 High Street, Saffron Walden, Essex, CB10 1AA, Tel: 01799 508608

Thought starters

- Have you defined the core areas in which you need to excel?
- Do routine and support functions consume an ever larger slice of overheads?
- Can you identify benchmark organisations to track their progress?
- Will outsourcing be an extension of your organisation's operations, or an innovation?

Disaster Planning

This checklist aims to help those putting together a disaster plan for their organisation. It covers physical disasters such as fire, flood, or terrorist attack.

Having a disaster plan means that many decisions are made before the disaster strikes, so that the first crucial days after the disaster are spent on dealing with the situation and not on deciding how to deal with it.

MCI standards

This checklist has relevance for the MCI Management Standards: Key Roles A and B – Manage Activities and Manage Resources.

Definition

A disaster plan (DP) aims firstly to prevent or reduce the likelihood of a disaster by identifying threats and taking the necessary preventative action, and secondly to ensure that the organisation is prepared to deal with an emergency effectively.

Benefits of disaster planning

In the event of a disaster, a DP:

- supports continuity of operations
- mitigates the financial consequences.

Drawbacks of disaster planning

- Poor planning or an out-of-date plan may be worse than no plan at all.
- The planning process can be time-consuming.

Action checklist

1. Establish a disaster planning team

This team should include staff responsible for personnel, buildings, public relations and IT as well as someone with general management responsibility.

You may want to include an external adviser with experience of disaster planning. The appointment of a team leader and a deputy is vital. Senior management should make their commitment to the DP clear to members of the team.

Ensure that the needs of staff and other groups such as customers are taken into account. Identify and prioritise those activities necessary to business continuity – consulting staff throughout the organisation will help to establish a sense of ownership and commitment.

2. Carry out a risk assessment

Identify especially vulnerable aspects of your particular industry, operation or service and determine potential risks, both internal and external, for your organisation. Assess and analyse these and then act to eliminate or reduce them. Distinguish between areas needing immediate action (the repair of broken windows for example) and those which can be dealt with over a longer period (such as the installation of a burglar alarm or sprinkler system). List the extra resources required for these. Consider appointing a loss adjuster in advance so that the insurance claim process can start immediately in the event of a disaster.

Check and seek professional advice where necessary on:

- insurance cover – is the existing cover adequate?
- maintenance of buildings and equipment
- security – do the detection and alarm systems work? If you don't have any, should you consider installing them?
- safety and fire precautions
- storage systems – are important documents held securely? Is adequate off-site storage available for IT back-ups?

3. Draw up a disaster plan

The DP should be simple and easy to understand yet contain all necessary information. It must be developed with the worst case scenario in mind but be flexible enough to be used in less severe cases. Try to obtain examples of other companies' disaster plans and learn from these. Remember that the recovery from the disaster could take twelve months or longer.

The personnel issues to be identified in the DP:

- key personnel – ensure out-of-hours contact details, on a rota basis if necessary, are available
- their responsibilities and limits of authority
- a control centre for the team, preferably off-site.

The DP should contain:

- priorities to be dealt with
- floor plans
- evacuation procedures
- precautionary measures
- details of where further information can be found
- procedures for jobs to be done during the recovery period
- a directory of suppliers, to provide equipment and supplies for use in emergency.

Anticipate the effects on employees, customers, suppliers and others. Consider:

- employees

  - Make sure managers have employees' telephone numbers and addresses at home so that they are able to contact them out of work hours.
  - Be prepared to offer counselling and other help to deal with the after-effects of a disaster.
  - Communicate with staff – over-communicate if necessary – about progress, moving back into the building, safety, etc. Make sure staff know whom to contact if there's a problem.
  - Make alternative arrangements for paying staff if routine mechanisms go out of action.

- alternative premises

  - Investigate a reciprocal arrangement for space with other organisations.

- continuity of operations and the level of service to be provided – the organisation needs to be operational as soon as possible, preferably the next day

  - Inform customers and suppliers and let them know where you can be contacted – customers will desert you if you are unavailable for weeks.
  - Brief the public relations spokesperson to deal with the media.

- physical communications

  - Investigate your telephone company's services – can they forward calls?
  - Plan for an ad hoc telephone directory and make sure your switchboard personnel know what to tell callers.
  - Decide where mail should be sent to.

- equipment and resources
  - Identify critical documents and their location so that vital material can be retrieved from the damaged building.
  - Store back-ups of material, including IT back-ups, off-site.
  - Work out what resources are needed during the recovery period and ensure these will be available.
  - Make sure cash is available at all times, but don't rush out and buy new equipment straight away – hiring may be a better option.
  - Investigate the possibility of establishing a resource network and identify cooperative partners with whom equipment, storage and costs could be shared.

Keep copies of the DP in a number of locations.

4. Test the plan with a pilot group

This will help to spot whether anything has been overlooked and give an indication of whether the plan would work in practice. How long does it take to set up the control centre? Will the communication systems work, even in the event of a natural disaster? Are the alternative premises suitable? Amend the plan as necessary to take into account any problems revealed by the pilot.

5. Communicate and implement the plan

A presentation should be made by a member of the disaster planning team to ensure all staff are aware of and understand the DP, its objectives and what to do in an emergency. Training will be an on-going process with new staff, and 'rehearsals' of emergency drills and reaction procedures should be carried out at least once a year to serve as a reminder for existing staff. Deal with any worries staff may have.

6. Monitor, revise and improve the plan

The DP is not set in stone – it should change with the circumstances. At intervals, at least annually, test out both individual components and the whole plan, and revise as necessary, taking into account impacts of new developments, such as new technology. Review reported disasters to see what can be learned to benefit your DP. Communicate any changes to staff.

Dos and don'ts for disaster planning

Do

- Be prepared.
- Learn from others' mistakes – and successes.
- Involve staff.
- Ensure all staff are aware of the plan.
- Communicate – with staff, customers, suppliers.
- Keep copies of the plan in a number of locations – it is no use if the plan itself is destroyed in the disaster!

Don't

- Be complacent – what if it did happen to you?
- Assume you've thought of everything – listen to comments and suggestions.
- Think of disaster planning as a one-off task – the plan must be kept up-to-date.

Useful reading

BOOKS

Disaster planning for library and information services, John Ashman, London: Aslib, 1995
Continuity planning: preventing, surviving and recovering from disaster, Ronald D Ginn, Oxford: Elsevier Advanced Technology, 1989

JOURNAL ARTICLES

Disaster management: controlling the plan, Graham Matthews, Managing Information, vol 1 no 7/8, Jul/Aug 1994, pp24–27
Bracing for emergencies, Charlene Marmer Solomon, Personnel Journal, vol 73 no 4, Apr 1994, pp74–76, 78, 80–83
The disaster business, Malcolm Brown, Management Today, Oct 1993, pp42–44, 47–48
Disaster and its aftermath, Lillian Gorman and Kathryn D McKee, HR Magazine, vol 35 no 3, Mar 1990, pp54–55, 57–58

Thought starters

- Have you ever been involved in a disaster? What can you learn from that experience?
- If a disaster did hit your organisation, would it survive?
- What risks does your organisation face and what can be done to minimise them?
- Can you afford not to have a disaster plan? The costs of a disaster are not just financial – they include interruption to business, wasted time and lost opportunities.

Carrying Out Marketing Research

This checklist has been designed to explain the basic steps of marketing research.

The use of marketing research has become increasingly prevalent since the 1980s. This has partly happened as a result of the quality revolution that swept through many organisations. At the heart of the quality movement is the notion that organisations need to get close to customers; in order to get close to customers, they need to listen to what those customers really want. Marketing research is one of the main ways of finding this out.

MCI Standards

This checklist has relevance for the MCI Management Standards: Key Roles A and D – Manage Activities and Manage Information.

Definition

For the purposes of this checklist, market research and marketing research are interchangeable terms, that are used to define a data gathering and analysis process which aims to provide information on the sale of products or services, and the customers who buy them.

But the research process goes a lot further into the areas of:

- market size and key market sectors
- market brand shares
- identifying potential customers
- identifying needs that may not have been articulated
- information on competitors
- defining actual and potential market sizes.

While there is much that marketing research can do, mostly it is directed towards discovering which groups or market sectors will buy your product, and what improvements, replacements or new related products may be desirable.

There is a range of different methodologies for carrying out marketing research – surveys, questionnaires, High Street or door-to-door interviews or discussion groups.

Advantages of carrying out marketing research

Effective marketing research can help organisations to:

- direct their energies towards the real needs of customers
- avoid wasting money on developing a product customers don't want
- develop a real customer focus and keep in touch with customers – the information gathered by marketing research is vital for developing the organisation's corporate strategy
- obtain a snapshot of what customers, or potential customers, feel and think at any particular time.

Issues to remember when carrying out marketing research

- If you don't define clearly what you want to find out, then the results you get back are likely to be unhelpful.
- What you get back will be the results of research, not necessarily reliable intelligence, with no guarantee of accuracy.
- Marketing research can be time-consuming and expensive.

Action checklist

1. Be clear about the purpose of the marketing research

How will you use the results? For instance to:

- develop performance indicators?
- develop standards?
- develop new products or services?
- discontinue or adapt product lines?
- improve quality?
- increase market share?

2. Decide what you want to find out

All too often marketing research fails because people aren't clear exactly what they want to find out. Hold a brainstorming meeting with the key people within your organisation to establish objectives for the research. A golden rule is that you should not try to cover too much in one exercise.

3. Be clear about who your customers are

The key stage of any marketing research is to decide whom it is you want to question. List all the types of customers you either have at the moment, or would like to appeal to, and target these people with your marketing research. Desk research – ie pulling together all the existing information you can find to help make some preliminary deductions – can be really helpful here.

4. Develop a brief

The brief is a clear statement of what is expected, by when and at what price. The brief will require you to:

- be specific on the particular market objectives at which the research is aimed
- describe any background information that can make a significant contribution
- suggest ideas on methods to be explored
- specify deadlines for delivery
- indicate requirements on confidentiality, disclosure and presentation
- indicate a date to take the brief forward (with shortlisted candidates if appointing an external agency).

If the research is to be done in-house, the brief is a key document. If you are going to select an external agency, it becomes essential.

5. Decide who's going to carry out the marketing research

If your organisation does not have a marketing research department (or sometimes, even if it does), you may need to bring in a specialist organisation to help you. If you feel you need to call in outside help, ask the following questions:

- What budget do you have? How much expert advice can you afford?
- How much time can you devote to the research?
- How much expertise do you have? Marketing research is a science as well as a skilled art.
- Do you have the resources? These include computer processing capability and statistical expertise as well as research experience.

6. Select an external agency

Find the names of suitable agencies through the trade press or trade association, directories, or contacts and recommendations. Establish some selection criteria, in addition to price, appearance and promise, such as reputation, membership of a professional body, track record, customer list, and any conflict of interests. Circulate your brief and shortlist candidates from their responses.

7. Choose your method

There are two main types of research, each of which has its own individual methods.

Qualitative research usually involves smaller groups than quantitative research. This is particularly useful when you are dealing with sensitive issues. In qualitative research, the questions are usually open, and concentrate on feelings. Qualitative research is not good for considering trends over a wide section of the community; it is better at helping you to flesh out the main issues.

In many ways, people see qualitative research as an effective way of getting insight into the way people feel and think. There are a number of methods involved in qualitative research. These include face-to-face interviews, taped interviews, telephone interviews, postal surveys and group discussions.

You may want to use more than one method: postal surveys, for example, can deal with large numbers superficially, while group discussions deal with small numbers in depth. There is often an inverse relationship between validity (whether you are measuring exactly what you want to measure) and reliability (whether the results are likely to be reproducible).

Quantitative research works mainly through the use of surveys carried out with a carefully selected sample of people and asks closed questions requiring specific answers such as:

- how much would you be prepared to pay?
- how satisfied were you?
- do you prefer this in blue, red or pink?

Quantitative research is useful because you can start putting percentage figures to your findings. In other words, if you ask a hundred people the same closed question, you can find out the percentage either agreeing or disagreeing.

8. Think about data analysis

As you put your research instrument together, think how you are going to store, sort and analyse the data contained in the returns. Think about ease of data entry, how any statistical or decision support package will manipulate the data, and how not to become a slave to a particular technique. Your results will need interpretation and understanding even if sophisticated techniques have been used. Remember that there are lies, damned lies and then there are statistics. Be wary of making sweeping assumptions from low returns but do look for the significant differences and relationships.

Marketing research sometimes throws up unexpected findings that shed new light on the issue. Be alert to the possibility of such findings when looking at the data and cross-analyses you want to perform.

Dos and don'ts for carrying out marketing research

Do

- Take time to plan research.
- Decide which kind of research is appropriate for you.
- Be clear about what you want to find out.
- Be prepared for surprises.

Don't

- Rush to start the research or jump to conclusions with the results.
- Ignore the results.
- Think marketing research is something you only do once – it should be ongoing.

Useful reading

Using market research to grow your business: how management obtain the information they need, Robin J Birn, London: Pitman, 1994

Successful market research in a week, Matthew Housden, London: Hodder & Stoughton, 1998

Understanding and designing market research, John R Webb, London: Academic Press, 1992

A handbook of market research techniques, Robin Birn, Paul Hague and Phyllis Vangelder, New York: Prentice Hall, 1990

Useful addresses

Chartered Institute of Marketing, Moor Hall, Cookham, Maidenhead, Berkshire SL6 9QH, Tel: 01628 427500

Market Research Society, 15 Northburgh Street, London EC1V 0AH, Tel: 0171 490 4911

Thought starters

- How well do you really know what your customers want?
- Do you really need to carry out marketing research?
- Which method is most appropriate to you – qualitative or quantitative research?
- Have you got a good source of advice for finding out which type of marketing research would suit your purposes?

Planning a Conference

This checklist is for those who are responsible for planning a conference. Conferences can be productive and memorable if they achieve the objectives of both the organisation and the delegates. Alternatively, they can be disorganised, the material irrelevant and a waste of delegates' time. The difference between the two is careful and detailed planning of the whole process, from the setting of objectives to the studious observation of protocol at the final dinner. If any detail is left to chance, and something goes wrong as a result, then the conference will be a failure for someone, and this can rebound on the organisers and the host organisation.

MCI Standards

This checklist has relevance for the MCI Management Standards: Key Role A – Manage Activities.

Definition

Conferences are held for many varied reasons – promotional, in-company, educational or sales based, to name a few. This checklist concentrates on conferences run for profit.

Basically a conference is a gathering of speakers and delegates meeting to solve particular problems, take specific decisions, discuss or learn about issues of mutual interest, publicise services to potential markets, or discuss cooperation with other bodies.

Action checklist

1. Establish the need for a conference

If you have never organised a conference before, be warned; relative to some other methods of achieving your objectives planning a conference can be very expensive and time-consuming. Ask yourself:

- whom you want to reach
- what you want to say, ask or discuss, and why
- how and where you want to say it.

By answering these questions you will both determine whether a conference really is the most appropriate and cost-effective way of achieving your objectives, and establish an initial set of objectives for planning the conference itself.

2. Set up a committee to plan the conference

Conferences are best planned by a small committee, which will set detailed objectives and a business or promotional programme. Remember, however, that the committee needs to be action-oriented.

3. Appoint a Conference Manager

The conference manager, appointed by the committee, has ultimate responsibility for the success of the conference, and should have experience in dealing with people at all levels and a motivation for handling conferences. If he/she does not like this sort of job, they won't do it well. The conference manager should:

- understand every detail of what is required and cross check with the conference committee regularly
- have full authority to negotiate over venue and with external parties involved. Enquiries should be directed to the manager when there are questions to answer, problems to solve or decisions to take.

It is possible to engage the services of a professional conference organiser. Although this can be expensive, it can also prove not only desirable but also cost-effective for large or complex conferences.

4. Prepare a schedule

It takes time to organise a successful conference. Appropriate venues are often booked up a year or more in advance. Consequently, the Committee and Manager must work out a schedule which will allow sufficient time to book a suitable venue, find appropriate speakers and send out publicity. The Manager must also begin to think of the multitude of other considerations which accompany a conference, such as:

- access and parking
- comfortable space for an unknown (although targeted) number of delegates
- presentation equipment and visual aids
- accompanying exhibition (or not)
- information helpdesk
- access to phones, fax or email for delegates
- catering and special diets
- range of accommodation requirements.

5. Draw up a programme

The business programme (drawn up by the Committee) should meet your objectives completely. Identify a range of speakers who should be experienced, sincere and convincing. Remember that poor presentation of first-class material can destroy a conference session. Plan the presentation schedule to ensure the attention of delegates is held (people usually concentrate for 25–30 minutes maximum before needing a break). In the programme make an allowance for:

- breaks between presentations
- extended refreshment breaks
- light lunches to prevent delegates from dozing off in the afternoon session (if serving alcohol do so in moderation)
- a few light relief presentations sandwiched between heavier presentations
- the right balance between inter-active, lecturing and discussion sessions
- the right balance between work and leisure.

Draw up a social programme as it is to the organiser's and delegates' advantage to remain together most, if not all, of the time.

6. Approach and book speakers

From the list of possible speakers identified, approach and confirm a booking with each of them as soon as possible. Once the booking is confirmed, agree the content and format of each speaker's presentation. Approach and book reserve speakers too, in case of last minute problems.

Remember to stress – and re-stress – the timing of the presentations as most speakers overrun. At least one dress rehearsal is advisable – schedule a date and ensure the speakers can attend.

7. Identify your delegates

The choice of delegates is closely linked to the conference objectives and is not quite as straightforward as might be imagined. A sales conference, for example, will have salespeople as its delegates, but who else will attend? Will you invite partners? Who will help educate your salesforce – the marketing department? Technical people? External consultants? Will you invite customers or potential customers?

8. Select a venue

Once the format of the conference, the speakers and the intended delegates have been determined, the Conference Manager should provide a list of suitable venues which fall within the financial guidelines set by the committee. Venues can be identified through personal knowledge, word of mouth or through placement agencies. Decide whether you want a venue from which people can escape (eg London) or in the middle of the country.

The venues must be visited by the Manager to compare them and ensure they meet all specifications. It is worth remembering that hotels provide special all-in conference rates and are often cheaper off-season and at weekends. More recently, universities have come into their own as conference venues. Many have upgraded Hall of Residence accommodation to provide comfortable, if not lavish, accommodation.

When making the visit the Manager will obviously be given the VIP treatment. Every opportunity should therefore be taken to observe the treatment other guests are receiving. If necessary, take up references from other organisations which have held conferences there.

The conference room is of prime importance. Size of room is the obvious first consideration, but in addition it should have:

- pleasant overall surroundings
- ceiling height in proportion to the size of room (a low ceiling can depress delegates)
- first class PA system (if the system is inadequate suitable equipment should be hired)
- efficient but quiet air-conditioning
- efficient black-out
- easy access for frequent exits and entrances
- comfortable seating.

Have a look in the bedrooms, both standard and executive, to check that they are clean and have the facilities your delegates will expect.

Are the catering facilities adequate to cope with the number of delegates who will be attending? Ask for some sample menus. Look at the dining area.

Check how the hotel will deal with the sudden arrival and departure of your delegates. Ask how they will deal with people who arrive at 2.00 am. A separate conference reception desk can deal with this problem efficiently and this can also serve as a conference enquiry desk throughout. Are leisure facilities available?

9. Advertise the conference

Now you have clear information on who you wish to attend and details of the venue and speakers it is essential to advertise the conference as widely, or as accurately, as possible. The Committee should have identified possible advertisers at an early stage.

10. Assemble a delegate information pack

As soon as arrangements allow, registered delegates should be sent a pre-conference pack containing details of:

- objectives of the conference and an outline of the programme
- arrival instructions
- hotel details (telephone number, map etc)
- details of what delegates are expected to pay
- name of the conference manager and assistant.

11. Get the atmosphere right

Getting the right atmosphere is vital, although there are no formulae for it. Panic and last-minute rush are obviously to be avoided; calm efficiency, courtesy, friendliness should be aimed for. Even a very well planned conference can flop if the atmosphere isn't right.

12. Debrief after the conference

During the conference, the Manager must concentrate solely on the administration of the event and the domestic needs of the delegates. The Conference Manager should have an assistant and sufficient other staff support.

Finally, those involved should hold a briefing. Was your conference a success, what lessons have you learned? Add any action points to your checklist for the next conference.

Dos and don'ts for the Conference Manager

Do
- Pay attention to details and re-check them with all concerned.
- Have contingency plans to deal with unexpected problems such as illness or guest speakers who are unavoidably delayed.
- Be a perfectionist to the extent of being a nuisance. If your conference fails on account of an avoidable error, you could be worse off than you were before you decided to hold it.
- Plan to collect feedback from delegates for analysis and review.

Don't
- Leave things to chance or assumption.
- Be afraid to make changes or deviate from the plan when the conference will benefit, or survive, as a result of such action.

Useful reading

BOOKS

How to organize a conference, Iain Maitland, Aldershot: Gower, 1996

The complete conference organiser's handbook, Robin O'Connor, London: Piatkus, 1994

JOURNAL ARTICLES

How to choose a conference venue, Alan Fowler, People Management, vol 2 no 7, 4 April 1996, pp40–41

Meeting points, Lucie Carrington, Personnel Today, 19 April 1994, pp35–36

Hangovers are out and cost-effectiveness is in, David Churchill, Management Today, January 1993, pp56–58

Effective Communications: Preparing Presentations

This checklist is intended for those who are required to give any form of presentation. It covers all the stages of preparing a talk, from accepting the invitation to checking the venue: the delivery of the presentation itself is covered in the next checklist (Effective Communications: Delivering Presentations). This checklist concentrates on how to develop an effective personal style rather than on the preparation of visual aids.

MCI Standards

This checklist has relevance for the MCI Management Standards: Key Role D – Manage Information.

Definition

For the purposes of this checklist, a presentation covers any talk to a group, whether formal or informal, from giving a team briefing to delivering a major speech: the same rules and principles apply.

Action checklist

1. Decide whether to accept

Ask yourself whether you are the right person to deliver this presentation. Do you have enough time to prepare? You may need to allow between 30 and 60 minutes for every minute of delivery. Are you excited enough about the topic to be enthusiastic? Do you know enough to answer awkward questions? If not, say no!

2. Clarify the details

Find out how long you will speak for and the exact subject. Will there be questions at the end? If there are other speakers, what will they cover, and how will you fit in with them?

3. Research your audience

View the audience as your customers. Try to gain a notion of their expectations: do they want to be informed, amused or challenged? How many will there be; what is their level and background; do they have any prior knowledge?

4. Define the purpose

Tailor the presentation to meet the audience needs you identified. Is the aim of the presentation to:

- persuade – a sales pitch
- instruct – if you know your topic
- inspire – as part of a change programme
- entertain – if you are naturally funny.

5. Assemble your material

Assemble anything relevant to your topic: ideas; articles; quotes; anecdotes; references. Accumulate the material over time but don't attempt to organise it while you collect it.

6. Organise your material

Review your collection. Group items into themes and topics. Are there metaphors or analogies which keep appearing?

7. Prepare an 'essay plan'

Structure the material into a rough plan. Aim for a beginning, a middle and an end.

8. Write a rough draft

Use the essay plan to sketch a first draft. Write without stopping and don't impose a structure while writing. Aim to tell the audience what you are going to say: tell them and end by summarising what you have told them. Try to make only five key points and a maximum of seven.

9. Edit the draft

Sleep on your first draft. Review it the following day. Convert the written word to speech: make the text more concrete, simpler and more illustrative. Use anecdotes. Shorten all your sentences and eliminate non-essential ideas and words. Cut any jargon or explain any that is unavoidable. Make sure the timing is right – speaking to an audience is slower than talking to a friend.

10. Refine the draft

Run through the draft several times, preferably in front of someone. Seek feedback and criticism on content, style and delivery. Ask your listener not to interrupt but to make notes.

11. Select your prompts

If you want or need to deliver a spontaneous presentation, run through the draft again and begin to highlight prompts – key words and phrases. These will be the basis of your script and perhaps your visual aids. Practise using the prompts alone and learn the thoughts behind the words. When you are confident, transfer the prompts to numbered cards. Continue practising and reducing the number of key words. (Sometimes, you will need to use a full script, for example, if the press are present, or if the occasion is very formal).

12. Select appropriate presentation aids

Presentation aids need to:

- be integrated – flow from your natural style
- move the presentation on – add value to it and be clearly relevant to content, or summarise what you are saying thus dispensing with a script
- be professional – clear, readable and consistent
- be appropriate in tone – full colour slides may not be right for a small informal group
- be simple to understand – clearly legible from the back of the room
- be graphic where appropriate – use symbols, drawings and charts to reinforce your words.

An increasing range of presentation aids, from flip charts and overhead transparencies to multimedia and computer generated graphics, is available.

13. Rehearse

Practise in your head, in front of a mirror or in front of a partner – he or she will be your sternest critic! Note any mannerisms you need to correct or anything you need constantly to remind yourself of as you talk: 'Don't put your hands in pockets!'. 'Smile!'. Keep these on a cue card when you give the presentation.

14. Check the venue

Sit where the audience will sit and check your visuals are visible. Sit or stand where you will deliver the presentation and check you can work the equipment. Can you use the microphone?

Dos and don'ts for preparing effective presentations

Do

- Practise as much as possible. Seek feedback and be open to criticism.
- Constantly review the purpose of your presentation against the text: are you meeting the customer's expectations?
- Remember that thorough preparation is a key factor in minimising nerves and ensuring a successful presentation.
- Put some enthusiasm into your presentation – stimulate the audience.

Don't

- Sit in a room with a blank sheet of paper and try to write: look for external stimuli.
- Use a visual aid just because it is funny or striking and you can't bear to leave it out.
- Take anything for granted: the topic; the audience; the extent of their knowledge; the venue; the equipment.

Useful reading

Successful presentation in a week, 2nd ed, Malcolm Peel, London: Hodder & Stoughton, 1998

I hate giving presentations: your essential confidence booster, Michael D Owen, Ely: Fenman, 1997

Making successful presentations, Patrick Forsyth, London: Sheldon Press, 1995

Successful Presentations, Carole McKenzie, London: Century Business, 1993

The Perfect Presentation, Andrew Leigh and Michael Maynard, London: Century Business, 1993

Janner's Complete Speechmaker, 4th ed, Greville Janner QC MP, London: Business Books Ltd UK, 1991

Thought starters

- Have you agreed to speak just because you were asked: if so, do you really know and care enough about the topic to excite your audience?
- Are you trying to convey too much information in one presentation? Your audience will only absorb a maximum of seven key points.

Effective Communications: Delivering Presentations

This checklist is intended for anyone giving a presentation, whether formal or informal. It assumes that you have spent time in preparing an effective presentation (see the previous checklist Effective Communications: Preparing Presentations) and are now ready to deliver it.

MCI Standards

This checklist has relevance for the MCI Management Standards: Key Role D – Manage Information.

Definition

For the purposes of this checklist, a presentation covers any talk to a group, whether formal or informal, from giving a team briefing to delivering a major speech: the same rules and principles apply.

Action checklist

1. Choose the right style

The size of your audience and the purpose of the presentation will determine its style. Obtain precise information about audience size: a large audience for one presenter is but a small group to another.

- For five to ten, aim for an informal style with few visual aids. Sit or balance on the edge of a table or desk. Plan to establish relationships immediately and engage each individual.
- For ten to thirty, you need a more formal style but you can still establish relationships. Stand up and expect to use some visual aids.
- For thirty to a hundred, you will need good presentation aids and a formal style; it will be difficult to engage with individuals.
- Over a hundred, view this as a theatre style presentation: you will be 'on stage' and performing with a microphone. Your facial gestures and body language will need to be exaggerated to be effective.

2. Check the venue

Do a last minute check on equipment: can you use the microphone, the projector, are your visual aids visible? Who will introduce you and when? Is there a glass of water to hand?

3. Check your appearance

Ensure your appearance doesn't detract from your message. Dress conservatively and tidily. Check your tie, shoes, make-up.

4. Establish your presence

Once you have been introduced, pause; take a deep breath; look at the audience; make eye contact and acknowledge their presence. Relax your body and stand tall. Smile!

5. Establish your credentials

Explain why you are there and what gives you the authority to speak. Confirm the audience's expectations by announcing what you will speak about. Resolve any confusions or queries immediately: it is always possible you are in the wrong place!

6. Involve your audience

Get their attention initially using a visual aid or something unexpected. Ask a question, even if it is rhetorical. Say something that shows you understand their concerns or expectations. Deflecting attention to the audience removes some of the attention from you and helps with stage fright.

7. Let your personality show

Remember that feelings, not facts, convince people. Put genuine conviction behind what you are saying and allow your emotions to show through. This will also help you to overcome stage fright.

8. Use positive body language

Remember to stand erect. Don't lean on the lectern and don't play with your hair, tie, jewellery or clothing. For those who talk better on the move, walk around naturally and use your hands as you would in conversation for emphasis. Use ordinary facial expressions and, where appropriate, smile!

9. Take control of your voice

Project your voice through standing straight and breathing deeply. Speak clearly and more slowly than usual. Speak naturally but lower the pitch of your voice if you are nervous. Be aware of your speech mannerisms and consciously avoid repeating them. Avoid hesitating: if you have lost your place or your nerve, just pause, but don't 'um' or 'er'.

10. Introduce variety

Vary the timing of your delivery and the pitch of your voice. Speed up or slow down and change tone in different sections. Use inflections and emphases even if they sound exaggerated to you. Occasionally pause or stop completely in a long presentation – the audience need time to absorb the content and you need time to reflect: are you going too quickly; have you put your hands in your pockets without realising it?

11. Build on your rapport with the audience

Maintain eye contact and play to the cheerleaders – people you know or sense to be sympathetic. Show how your presentation is relevant to them and avoid using 'I' or 'me' too often.

12. Introduce humour

If you are confident, use humour to lighten or vary the mood. Use it only to support the text, not in its own right. Don't be cruel to anyone in the audience.

13. Face up to the unexpected

The audience will notice disturbances or mistakes but you will only remember how you handled them. Acknowledge rather than ignore interruptions and try to deflect or make light of them through humour.

14. Improvise

Although thorough preparation is essential it may be inappropriate to come over as too 'prepared', slick or clinical. Remember to adjust to the mood and atmosphere of the audience.

15. Conclude

Bring the presentation to a conclusion. Be brief, don't repeat the main text and end on a high, in tone, energy and content. Leave the audience wanting slightly more.

16. Be positive about questions

Actively encourage questions. Repeat the question so everyone can hear it. If you don't know the answer, admit it but offer to take a name and address to reply to later. Don't get into debate or argument.

Dos and don'ts for delivering effective presentations

Do
- Be yourself: allow your own personality to come through rather than trying to emulate presenters you admire.
- Start and finish on time – or before time if there are to be questions – otherwise you will lose the audience's sympathy regardless of how good the content is.
- Use handouts to convey detailed or complex ideas rather than cramming them into your presentation.

Don't
- Try to cover too much in one presentation and end up rushing to finish by talking faster.
- Use humour inappropriately or use it against your audience: you are the only legitimate target in the room.
- Use too many visual aids: they distract the audience and rarely add value.

Useful reading

Successful presentation in a week, 2nd ed, Malcolm Peel, London: Hodder & Stoughton, 1998

I hate giving presentations: your essential confidence booster, Michael D Owen, Ely: Fenman, 1997

Making successful presentations, Patrick Forsyth, London: Sheldon Press, 1995

The perfect presentation, Andrew Leigh and Michael Maynard, London: Century Business, 1993

Successful presentations, Carole McKenzie, London: Century Business, 1993

Janner's complete speechmaker, 4th ed, Greville Janner QC MP, London: Business Books Ltd, 1991

Thought starters

- Does each part of the content of your speech match up to the title and purpose?
- Do all your visual aids really add something to the spoken word?
- Have you tried your presentation out on guinea pigs for length, humour or interest?
- Have you ever used the particular visual aid you will be working with before?
- Do you know who your audience will be or how many there will be?

Effective Visual Aids

This checklist is intended to assist those who wish to use visual aids in a presentation, whether formal or informal, to a group, large or small.

MCI Standards

This checklist has relevance for the MCI Management Standards: Key Roles B and D – Manage Resources and Manage Information.

Definition

For the purpose of this checklist, visual aids are images, either still or moving, that are used to enhance a presentation. They include films, overhead transparencies, models, product samples and handouts.

Advantages of using visual aids

Used in conjunction with the trainer's words, visual aids help the learner to retain the information better than by just listening to the words.

Visual aids can be used to:

- explain, amplify, simplify or clarify points
- hold attention, help concentration and aid retention
- add interest and variety, and help break up an event into smaller sections.

If a picture is worth a thousand words, then visual aids can save time as well.

Disadvantages of using visual aids

The only real drawback to using visual aids is that, if their use is not planned and relevant to the presentation, then they can detract from the learning points.

Action checklist

1. Define the purpose of the presentation

Consider what objectives you want to achieve with the presentation – for example to give the audience a broad overview of a subject, or a more detailed technical understanding of a subject, or perhaps a mixture of both.

2. Draw out the key points

Ascertain what the key points are that you want to make in the presentation. Are you trying to put across too much information in one go? Does each key point need to be reinforced with one or more aids? How many secondary points would also benefit from the use of visual aids? Too many secondary points may distract from the key features that you want to emphasise.

3. Analyse the audience

You should already have a good idea of the likely audience. Consider its level of knowledge – will it be made up mainly of experienced senior executives, professionals, technicians, students, the general public, company staff, or a mixture? This level of knowledge will affect the level of detail and difficulty of the subject that you wish to transfer, and it will also help you to decide on the most suitable visual aids. Some graphs, for example radar diagrams, need prior knowledge of their structure and layout to be understood and so may not be suitable for a lay person.

4. Consider content and format

What is the most suitable format to gain maximum understanding and clarity of the key points? Text may be suitable for many occasions, either as complete paragraphs, short individual sentences or 'bullet points'. Graphical displays can be computer generated and include drawings, diagrams, graphs or charts (bar, pie, vertical, horizontal), or photographs. Some topics may be better explained using films or videos; others, for example marketing presentations, may require models or samples to be effective. Make certain that all visual aids are fully legible from the back of the room you will be using (how often have you heard 'You won't be able to read all the figures, but I'll put this table up all the same'?)

Remember, whatever the presentation, that:

- visual aids can be used in combination (and can be even more effective used this way)
- colour should be used sparingly for maximum impact (black on white is clearest for text)
- excessive detail in each image will cause confusion
- it may be necessary to break complex issues into several images, but it should be shown how they 'fit' together.

5. Think about the equipment to be used

First, find out what equipment is available. Remember that, if a booking system is in operation in your organisation, you may not have access to a particular piece of equipment on the day of the presentation. Check on availability well in advance.

There is a wide range of equipment that can be used, both traditional and high-tech, including:

Whiteboards and flipcharts

These are generally blank at the beginning of the session and are written on as the presentation is made. If they are to be prepared beforehand, make sure they can be covered (more difficult with a whiteboard than a flipchart) when not being referred to, so that they don't distract the audience. Electronic whiteboards are now available which allow a printed copy to be made for a handout, but these are expensive.

Overhead transparencies (OHTs)

These can be used in conjunction with an overhead projector (OHP) to produce a large image onto a wall or screen. They can be hand-prepared during the session or pre-printed, and have the advantage of being reasonably cheap. Several transparencies can be overlaid to build up an image. Projector fans can be noisy so OHPs should be switched off when not in use.

Slide or filmstrip projectors

These are normally used when high quality images are involved. Slides are fiddly to load (although some machines allow a number of slides to be inserted in advance of the session) and need a darkened room for the image to be seen properly.

Films and videos

Film is less popular now than video, but can still be an excellent medium for presentations. Videos can be viewed on normal-sized television sets or, using appropriate projection systems, on larger screens. Both videos and films, as well as being expensive, go out-of-date, so their use should be carefully planned.

Other electronic projection equipment

A range of equipment that allows the enlarged display of information held in a PC is available and is worth investigating with local suppliers.

Remember to make sure that you know how to operate the equipment before you make a presentation. You may be required to enlarge, reduce or focus images. If you don't know how, then ensure that a trained person is available to help.

6. Prepare or hire the visual aids

Are any prepared aids already available in-house? Could you use these? If not, consider who is to produce or hire them – should it be yourself, your own department, the reprographics department, or an outside firm, for example?

Is there a house style to follow? Even if not, ensure that there is a uniform layout for all the aids.

Photographs, videos and slides can all be purchased or hired from specialist agencies.

Allow sufficient time for production, including any corrections, additions, alterations, purchase or hiring arrangements.

Visual aids should be cost-effective, so take into account the costs in preparing the material, including the possible hire, leasing or purchase of equipment, such as projectors. If leasing or purchasing, consider maintenance, depreciation, replacement and insurance costs, including the cost of any service agreements. Hire costs, even for just one day, can be considerable.

7. Organise the venue

The expected number of persons present and the size of the room in relation to the maximum size of the image or other aids are factors that should be examined when selecting a venue. The layout of the seats – theatre style, semi-circle, or U-shaped – is important. What is the view like from the furthest seat? Try to ensure that neither you nor the equipment obscure anybody's view.

Make sure it is possible to darken the room if necessary in order for images to be seen. Where sound is needed, for example with video or film, make sure the equipment is adequate or obtain extra speakers.

8. Plan the use of the visual aids and rehearse the presentation

Carefully plan when to introduce the visual aids during the presentation. Two presentations are rarely ever the same, so you should identify the method of using the visual aid which suits your particular style. Is it better to introduce a topic and talk about it briefly before showing any visual aid, rather than displaying something 'cold' and then talking about it? Films can be shown and handouts made available at the beginning to act as a focus for the remainder of the presentation or at the end as a summary. Consider the pros and cons of each. Models or samples should be kept hidden from view until required. After each aid has served its purpose, remove it from view so that it does not distract the audience's attention, but remember to leave enough time for people to take notes if necessary. Provide handouts summarising the essential information presented.

Carry out a full rehearsal at least once, using all the aids, to ensure a smooth integration between the talking and the visual aids. Ask a friend or colleague for critical feedback – for example on how well each aid served its purpose. Use aids as your notes only if you are confident that you can do so. Remember not to turn your back on the audience when referring to an aid.

9. Make a final check

Ensure that all equipment has arrived and is in working order about an hour before the presentation. Try out slides or OHTs and make sure they are in the order in which they will be displayed. Any delay during delivery due to problems of this nature conveys an unprofessional and disorganised manner which will detract from the overall presentation. Ensure pens and other writing instruments are in good working order.

10. Have an alternative plan

If, in spite of all your careful planning, equipment breaks down, an alternative plan will enable you to carry on with the presentation.

Dos and don'ts for the effective use of visual aids

Do

- Make sure each visual aid or combination of aids is the best for the job.
- Try to find out about your audience.
- Make sure you are familiar with any equipment to be used.

Don't

- Display the visual aid for too long, as it will become a distraction.
- Put too much detail into each aid.
- Forget to rehearse the complete presentation at least once.

Useful reading

BOOKS

Making successful presentations, Patrick Forsyth, London: Sheldon Press, 1995

Successful presentations, Carole McKenzie, London: Century Business, 1993

Effective presentations, Anthony Jay, London: Pitman, 1993

Successful presentations in a week, 2nd ed, Malcolm Peel, London: Hodder & Stoughton, 1998

JOURNAL ARTICLES

Presentation systems – present and direct, George Cole, Accountancy, Vol 117 no 1232, April 1996, pp70–72

Using presentation aids, Nigel Gunn, Training Officer, Vol 26 no 12, December 1990, pp351–353

Make visual aids pull their weight, James F Carey, Journal of Management Consulting, Vol 5 no 3, 1989, pp25–31

Thought starters

- What are the best (worst) visual aids that you have seen used in a presentation? Why were they good (bad)?
- Which visual aid helps you understand or learn more easily?

This checklist provides guidance for those who wish to undertake a direct mail advertising campaign.

Information technology has allowed such campaigns to become increasingly sophisticated as an enormous amount of information can be collected, stored and retrieved on both industrial and private consumers. It is now possible to obtain highly specific lists of addresses on particular groups to which an organisation or individual can send direct mail to advertise their products or services. Companies are collecting information on their customers, ranging from their birthdays to their purchasing habits, so they can tailor a marketing message particular to each individual.

This one-to-one form of communication can be very effective, but to do it properly requires careful planning and designing. The scale of the direct mail campaign and the number of customers contacted will depend on the size of the organisation (ranging from single individuals to multi-national corporations) and the resources available; the procedure, however, remains the same.

MCI Standards

This checklist has relevance for the MCI Management Standards: Key Roles A and B – Manage Activities and Manage Resources.

Definition

Direct mail is a method of advertising a product or service using letters, cards or leaflets sent through the post and personally addressed to a selected list of individuals or organisations.

Advantages of direct mail

- Individuals are communicated with on a person-to-person level.
- Wastage is low as targeted individuals are carefully selected.
- Effectiveness is easily and quickly measured.
- Initial testing is easy (by sending out to a sample of addresses).

Disadvantages of direct mail

- People are often wary of/uninterested in unsolicited ('junk') mail – many hate it.
- A suitable mailing list must be available – it can be expensive to research and build up a suitable list.
- An up-to-date and accurate mailing list is a relative rarity.

Action checklist

1. Define the terms of reference

Identify what you want to achieve by using direct mail. Is it, for example, a general awareness campaign or is it to help launch a new service or product? The target audience for the campaign should be defined. Are there sectors who do not use the service or product, or are there those who subscribe in larger quantities? Identify the profile of your best customers and you will identify the profile of your best prospects. Assign a budget for the campaign.

2. Decide who is to run the campaign

Appoint an agency to run the campaign. This may be your own marketing department if you have one which is large enough, or a special working party drawn from your organisation. Consider contracting the work out to an external consultant if you feel you lack the necessary expertise internally. This may prove to be more expensive, but a badly run campaign is not just ineffective, it can also be damaging to an organisation's reputation.

3. Prepare or obtain a mailing list

Evaluate the usefulness of the information on in-house databases. If there are limitations suggest improvements, or if an in-house database doesn't exist, consider the benefits and costs of starting one.

It will be much cheaper to purchase a mailing list from a specialist company. Make sure you check the company's reputation for producing lists. The addressee information must be up-to-date and accurate. Nobody likes receiving mail with their name misspelled or seeing the addressee as someone who moved 4 years ago, or two copies addressed to slightly different people. It is also a waste of money sending mail to someone for whom the product or service is totally irrelevant.

4. Design the mailing

Check out in-house capability of designing advertising material. Be creative when designing the mailing (including the envelope) to attract and hold the attention of the addressee. Make it look as personal as possible – many people bin computer-addressed envelopes on sight. Ensure that the design matches the type of target; for example, the style appropriate for teenagers will differ from that appropriate to senior managers. Consider contracting out the design stage to an appropriate agency if your organisation lacks expertise. Remember: it is more effective to mail a smaller number of professional looking documents that have incurred the additional expense of a design agency than a large number of cheaper, poorly designed in-house ones.

Where the addressee needs to get back in touch offer a stimulus for an early response, possibly a discount or free gift, as the longer a person leaves mail unanswered the less likely they are to bother. In cases which need a mailed response enclose a postage-paid envelope and don't ask for too much information; minimise the time and complexity involved to complete the form. Don't tell people they have been specially chosen for a gift, or that they might be one of a lucky sample to receive a gift – they are wise to this by now, having never ever had a gift, or if they have it is one that is binned.

It is often useful to produce two or three different designs to use in the testing stage. Check that everything will remain within the budget when reproduced on its full scale.

5. Test the mailing

Send out a copy of the mailing to a sample from the list (making sure your sample is large enough to yield valid results – the more you want to break it down into categories, the larger it needs to be). If more than one design of mailing was produced these should be tested. Evaluate the results by checking the time taken to reply, the information obtained, and subsequently the number of sales. Look for any sectors that have not replied, for example the younger age range.

6. Make modifications and produce the package

Make any necessary changes (which are identified from any confusion or doubts arising from the test) to the mailing and package. Have the final copy of the package printed to the numbers required.

7. Prepare for response

Plan for a maximum response. This may mean taking on additional staff temporarily or ordering greater levels of stock. Customers will not be happy if their order cannot be met and are told an item is sold out. Ensure staff are aware of the pending campaign and the possibility of a large response over a short period of time. Prepare to monitor increases in telephone calls, orders, or service usage.

8. Send out the mailing

Depending on the size of the mailing it is often sensible to outsource envelope-stuffing to an external agency. The size and importance of the mailing and the capability of existing resources and budgets will determine whether you need to take on temporary staff or not.

9. Evaluate the results

Look for the same pointers as in the test mailing, along with the capability of staff to cope with the increased workload. Check that the stimulus for early response worked. Compare the results of the campaign, for example numbers of extra sales, against the original objectives or targets. Overall, identify problem areas and ways that improvements could be made for next time. Make as much use as possible of the incoming data in order to improve your own customer databases and the profiles of order prospects.

Dos and don'ts for using direct mail

Do

- Use the most up-to-date and accurate mailing list you can obtain.
- Try to be innovative when designing your letter – but keep it short and to the point.
- Make sure the recipient knows what they have to do next.
- Offer a stimulus to reply quickly.
- Review the results and use them when planning future mailings.

Don't

- Send out the mailing without testing it on a sample first.
- Throw too much information at the addressee.
- Use language/terminology that the addressee will not understand.
- Forget that a successful campaign will increase the workload.

Useful reading

Books

Successful direct mail in a week, Liz Ferdi, London: Hodder & Stoughton, 1995

How to write letters that sell, Christian Godfrey and Dominique Glocheux, London: Piatkus, 1995

The Royal Mail direct mail handbook, Les Andrews (ed), Watford: Exley, 1988

Journal articles

How to write a letter that sells, Small Business Confidential, No 104, April 1992, pp8–10

It's in the post, Phil Churchill, Accountancy, Vol 104 no 1155, 1989, pp127–128

Making the most of mail campaigns, Winston Marsh, Australian Accountant, October 1989, pp28–31

Useful addresses

Direct Mail Department, Royal Mail Streamline, Streamline House, Sandylane West, Oxford, OX4 5ZZ, Tel: 01865 748768

Direct Marketing Association (UK) Ltd, Haymarket House, 1 Oxendon Street, London, SW1Y 4EE, Tel: 0171 321 2525

Setting up a Customer Care Programme

This checklist describes the stages in establishing an organisational framework that maximises the value offered to and derived from customers.

MCI Standards

This checklist has relevance for the MCI Management Standards: Key Roles A and G – Manage Activities and Manage Projects.

Definition

Successful customer care means making the customer want to come back for more, and getting them to recommend products and services to others. Customer care is not only about meeting customer expectations but 'delighting' the customer by focusing staff energies on offering value, getting it right first time, and yet improving it in the future.

Benefits of a customer care programme

A comprehensive customer care programme impacts on the organisation through:

- increased success
- a developing and satisfied workforce.

Drawbacks of a customer care programme

There can be no such thing as a zero customer care programme – to take no account of customers is to ignore the future of the business.

Action checklist

1. Secure top management commitment

Unless top management are fully committed to the concept of customer care, there is very little chance of success. A formalised customer care programme with involved leadership helps to focus roles and responsibilities in a clear manner.

2. Know your customers

Excellence in customer care is wholly reliant upon knowing your customers' needs and expectations. Needs are not the same as demands: people don't ask for what they don't expect to get, even when it could be provided. Anticipating real needs can give competitive advantage.

While it is important to remember that most organisations have internal customers in other departments, divisions and sectors, establishing external customers' needs can be a lot more complex. A range of approaches is available, including:

- feedback direct from customers and staff
- direct discussion with customers
- analysis of customer complaints, enquiries and thank-yous
- attitude surveys and questionnaires
- visits to premises
- focus-group discussions and customer audits.

3. Assimilate the major elements of customer care

Customer care is more than just an excellent product or a first-class service; it involves a host of elements that contribute to genuine care and value for the customer, such as, in the purchasing process:

- clarity of literature on product features, price, payment methods, availability and after-sales support
- the way the first contact takes place and is followed up
- simple ordering procedures highlighted by convenience for the customer
- prompt order processing
- prompt notification of any changes to specification or procedure
- clear invoicing with no hidden charges
- assistance when the product is delivered
- easy after-sales contacts.

4. Develop service levels

It may be the case that performance standards do exist but are not formalised, recorded or audited. It is not good enough to set indicators or levels which place supplier-convenience in front of customer-convenience; such levels should be worked out, discussed and agreed with customers. It is good to set levels which are challenging but have a realistic chance of attainment. Questions to help set service levels may include:

- How many times does the phone ring before someone answers?
- How many transfers take place before the customer gets an answer?
- How long does it take to process an order?
- How long does it take to respond to a complaint?

Measurements must not gain such a hold on processes that they become a time-consuming nuisance; they should be realistic and helpful in developing a relationship – however short-lived – between supplier and customer. Remember, what gets measured, gets done.

5. Recruit the right staff

Your service is only as professional as the people delivering it; attracting new customers and retaining existing ones are tasks for competent people. Focusing the recruitment process on customer care can mean introducing questions at the interview stage, covering, for example:

- candidates' experiences with customers
- service levels and customer expectations
- the prioritisation of customer needs over in-house organisational activities
- incentives to motivate front-line staff.

Remember to include customer care on the induction programme.

6. Get your communications right

Top management commitment to a customer care programme is no good if the right message is not conveyed to all staff in the right way. If internal communications are not working as well as they should, then external communications cannot be expected to be successful. Communications have to be reliable, consistent and regular so that all people receive the same message and interpret it in the same way so that the end results are the same.

7. Convert complainants back into customers

Prompt and sympathetic handling of complaints can turn a disgruntled customer into a happy – and longer-lasting – one. People whose complaints are fully dealt with are more loyal than those who have no complaints.

Often, those who receive the complaint are not at fault, yet they bear the brunt of customer dissatisfaction. It is vital that all staff are familiar and comfortable with the organisation's procedure so that they are prepared to receive complaints and to start converting the customer from dissatisfied to satisfied. Remembering that the complaint must be dealt with promptly, accurately – it may just be a misunderstanding or lack of information – and efficiently, individuals in the 'front line' need to be familiar with seven rules for dealing with verbal complaints:

- Listen patiently – let the customer air the grievance without interruption.
- Acknowledge the customer's viewpoint – even if you don't agree.
- Apologise – say sorry if a mistake has been made, but there's no need to overdo it.
- Find a solution – establish what needs to be done to rectify the problem.
- Keep the complainant informed – lack of ongoing information can exacerbate the problem.
- Reach a conclusion to resolve the problem for the customer quickly – a more permanent solution may take longer to find.
- Follow up – check that promised action happens.

8. Reward service accomplishments

Recognition and reward for superior performance helps with reinforcement. Try to recognise smaller accomplishments not just the major ones.

Customers too appreciate rewards for their loyalty, and such rewards will make a significant contribution to their retention.

9. Stay close to your customers

Staying close to customers means:
- carrying out continuous research in order to learn from them
- asking questions about the quality and performance of the product at regular intervals after the sale
- developing procedures to stay up-to-date with customer needs
- listening.

10. Train your people and work towards continuous improvement

Recruiting the right staff is just one of the first steps in a customer care programme. Training staff to understand customer needs and tackle customer problems, to turn threats into opportunities for the organisation, is also a prerequisite for effective and lasting customer care. Training them on a continuing basis, especially in friendly telephone and face-to-face techniques, which result in sincerity and substance rather than empty phraseology, can provide organisations with an advantage that will score with customers.

Providing feedback from customers is especially motivating for staff in 'backrooms', who are not in direct contact with customers. Feedback can make an important contribution to continuous improvements in not only how things are done but also what is done.

Dos and don'ts for setting up a customer care programme

Do

- Make recruitment and selection customer-oriented activities.
- Discuss customer levels of expectation with all staff.
- Analyse complaints to discern any trends or patterns.
- Offer incentives to encourage customers to give feedback.
- Stay close to your customers – the profile of your best prospect is the profile of your best customer.

Don't

- Forget to involve all staff in customer service discussions.
- Lose sight of your internal customers.
- Neglect to celebrate and publicise good news and achievements.
- Omit to record thanks as well as complaints.
- Say 'It isn't my fault', or 'I don't know who deals with that here'.

Useful reading

Successful customer care in a week, 2nd ed, John Wellemin, London: Hodder & Stoughton, 1998

Creating a customer focused company: 25 proven customer strategies, Ian Linton, London: Pitman, 1994

Perfect customer care, Ted Johns, London: Arrow, 1994

Raising the standard: a survey of managers' attitudes to customer care, Neville Benbow, Corby: Institute of Management, 1994

Keeping customers for life, Richard F Gerson, London: Kogan Page, 1992

Thought starters

- A service that receives no complaints may receive little else – a service that ignores complaints will receive less use.
- What irritates you as a customer of other organisations? What delights you?
- How can you:
  - improve ordering/purchasing convenience for your customers?
  - develop more direct relationships with your customers?
  - reward loyal customers?
  - recognise customer (dis)satisfaction?

Getting Close to the Customer

This checklist is aimed at managers at all levels and explores the steps and principles involved in assessing the needs of customers as the basis of any business operation. It focuses on how to find out the needs of customers but does not extend to suggesting ways of meeting those needs.

MCI Standards

This checklist has relevance for the MCI Management Standards: Key Role A – Manage Activities.

Definition

Getting close to the customer involves gathering facts and knowledge about your customers (both current and potential), and turning these into an awareness of what customers want from you and how they perceive your organisation and your products and services. This awareness must then be acted on to ensure that you continually meet customer demands and ensure long term survival and profitability.

Advantages of being close to your customers

Being close to your customers will enable you to:

- be more responsive to changes in demand and in the market
- act on facts rather than hunches or intuition
- develop a product or service better tailored to your target market
- achieve improved sales and increased profits.

Disadvantages of being close to your customers

The advantages far outweigh any disadvantages, but you should take the following factors into account:

- The better you try to get to know customers, the more you risk intruding on their privacy.

- If you are asking a customer to impart personal or valuable information, then you will probably have to offer a reward or benefit in return.
- Customers may resist telling you personal information, and may not always tell the truth.
- Surveys and research can be costly and time-consuming.

Action checklist

1. Examine the culture of your organisation

Closeness to your customers cannot occur successfully unless the culture of your organisation encourages such an attitude. All staff must think 'customer first' – staff who are not customer focused in their work may jeopardise the success of the organisation by making inappropriate decisions, failing to respond to changing situations quickly enough or in the right way, or neglecting to serve customers in a way which encourages their loyalty.

If the culture in your organisation does not facilitate the right attitudes, you will need to embark on a programme of long-term culture change to make this possible.

Remember that every section of your organisation has customers. Staff in direct support of external customers cannot provide effective service unless they are supported internally by colleagues along the chain. To encourage internal service departments to adopt an outward-looking customer focus, their operators could work for a week or two in the department they service.

Remember that customer focus must pervade all levels of the organisation. How often do key decision makers and strategy formulators in your organisation deal face to face with customers? A period on the front line would increase their awareness.

2. Identify your customers

Your customers are those who use the output of your work. They may be internal to your organisation (for example, the personnel function will have all organisational employees as its customers), or external (members of the public, other businesses, or government or public bodies). When identifying customers, remember to distinguish between those who pay for your product (for example, the parent who buys the toy), and those who use the product (the child).

In order to get close to your customers you will need to know who they are, and you will probably wish to compile a database of them so that you can create a profile of your customer base. Bear in mind that any recording of an individual's personal details must comply with the requirements of the Data Protection Act 1984.

3. Profile your customers

A wide range of factors influences customer behaviour and choices, for example:

- **gender** – particularly where the purchaser or end user is not the sole decision maker
- **age** – with different age ranges being susceptible to targeting by some products more than others
- **marital status** – especially combined with other factors such as children and disposable income
- **home ownership** – indicates specific needs and responsibilities which relate to buying patterns
- **location** – urban consumers differ from rural ones and regions differ culturally and economically
- **lifestyle** – all customers have individual activities, interests and opinions.

These factors become more useful when information from them is used in combination – for example, home ownership, age and number of dependent children can indicate likely amount of disposable income.

Decide how to approach your customers to find out their basic characteristics. It will probably not be possible to ask every customer individually, but there are nonetheless many approaches to follow, including:

- market research
- questionnaires
- user- or focus-group discussions
- customer audits
- attitude surveys.

Take advantage of opportunities to meet business customers at their premises or at yours in a series of open days or customer care programmes, through partnership situations arising out of new product development, through membership of user groups or industry liaison meetings.

4. Assess your customers' opinions and attitudes

If organisations have an inaccurate perception of customer needs, it is probably a result of:

- assumptions about what customers should think, which might be shattered if tested
- weak anecdotal evidence, where too much importance is attached to single incidents
- atypical complaints, where the opinions of small numbers of highly articulate customers may be accorded too much weight.

If you don't make the effort to find out what customers think, you can be caught off-balance when they go elsewhere. If you don't know why they are going elsewhere, you won't know what alternative actions to take. In addition to finding out basic factual information about who your customers are, you need to establish:

- why customers buy your product or use your service
- how they use it
- what their opinion is of the product or service
- why they choose your offering over others in the market
- what their experience is of the product or service in terms of performance and after-sales care.

Remember that attitudes and opinions are difficult to quantify, and that many factors will influence a decision to purchase or to remain loyal to your brand. Customers may be influenced as much (or more) by their impressions of service – courtesy, promptness, etc – as by the quality of your product. Detailed research will be needed to explore these areas, and if you do not have adequate in-house expertise you may wish to use an external research agency.

Be sure to listen to your front line staff. They will pick up first-hand comments from customers about their satisfaction and dissatisfaction, and you could set up a procedure for reporting this type of information.

Channels usually employed for support and after-sales care can also be used for ascertaining customer opinions by keeping the dialogue open in ways that are meaningful to the customer. Such ways include customer charters, extended warranties, statements (and monitoring) of performance standards, open and willing acceptance of penalties for non-compliance, and return of money in the case of non-satisfaction.

5. Take action on your findings

Analyse the results of your research, interpret the data you have gathered and publicise the findings. Having interpreted your data, you must work out where action is needed to maintain competitive advantage. Make sure that all staff are involved in this process, as everyone must think 'customer first'.

Ensure your attention to your customers' needs is long-term. For example, you could set up a regular research project or customer audit, introduce customer suggestion schemes with response mechanisms, or set up a scheme to constantly monitor your market.

6. Consider using the Internet to improve customer focus

The World Wide Web is an interactive medium which is being increasingly used to enable customers to select items for purchase, specify designs, and make comments and suggestions on products and services. The Web is beginning to offer an opportunity to change the traditional relationship between supplier and consumer, putting the consumer in the driving seat –

instead of companies marketing to consumers, the Web enables consumers to invite suppliers to make offers for service. Used judiciously, the Web can permit an organisation to get closer to its customers than ever before.

Remember, however, that not all your customers and potential customers will have access to the Internet, so any plans involving use of the Web will have to be considered carefully.

7. Give feedback to customers

Let your customers know that you have taken on board their needs and their ideas. This may mean publishing a new mission statement reiterating your commitment to fulfilling their needs, or it may involve publication of survey results and details of new products or product amendments made as a result of the research.

Feedback is not a one-off event – it needs to be a continuous process, informing customers of reactions to suggestions, mistakes and new ideas, and encouraging further comment.

Dos and don'ts for getting close to the customer

Do
- Think of ways of rewarding customers for sharing their likes and dislikes.
- Be aware that some may feel that getting close to the customer is tantamount to an intrusion of privacy.
- Make sure your organisational culture encourages staff to think 'customer first'.
- Integrate customer focus with other business activities – it should be a cross-departmental, cross-functional initiative.

Don't
- Make assumptions about what people think without checking them out.
- Fall into the trap of thinking that customers are stupid.
- Rely on data from too small a sample of customers.
- React too hastily to vociferous complainers – see if other customers feel the same.

Useful reading

Meeting customer needs, 2nd ed, Ian Smith, Oxford: Butterworth Heinemann, 1997

Connecting with your customers, Steve Morris and Graham Willcocks, London: Pitman, 1996

Successful customer care in a week, 2nd ed, John Wellemin, London: Hodder & Stoughton, 1998

Perfect customer care: all you need to get it right first time, Ted Johns, London: Arrow Books, 1994

Thought starters

- When was the last time you spoke to, or came into contact with, a customer?
- Do you know who buys your product and why?
- Do customers talk as much about competitor products as yours?
- How easy is it for your customers to complain and give feedback?

Handling Complaints

This checklist outlines a procedure for handling complaints in small or large, manufacturing or service, private or public sector organisations.

It is designed to enable a consistent organisation-wide approach to complaints which ensures that they are dealt with effectively to the advantage of both the customer and the organisation.

MCI Standards

This checklist has relevance for the MCI Management Standards: Key Role A – Manage Activities.

Definition

A complaint is an expression of lack of satisfaction with any product or service, whether orally or in writing, from an internal or external customer.

Advantages

A complaints procedure:

- provides a clear approach when a complaint occurs
- engenders understanding and confidence on how to tackle complaints
- helps to remove personal 'guilt' feelings when receiving a complaint
- leads to a recognition of complaints as valuable feedback, not criticisms
- can produce records for analysing possible service improvements.

Action checklist

1. Establish a common approach to handling complaints

This must have widespread approval from the top to the bottom of the organisation, including staff who do not come into direct contact with customers. Ensure that everyone is thinking about customers in the same way. This should be embedded into the organisation's culture and is primarily the responsibility of senior management.

Remember that when customers complain, they like to be:

- aware of who is dealing with the complaint
- listened to and believed
- treated fairly and efficiently
- kept informed of progress
- compensated if it is appropriate.

2. Draw up a standard complaints form

This is a valuable tool which should include the following sub-headings:

Receipt details
- date received
- received by
- department/division

Customer details
- name, address, identifier
- telephone / fax / e-mail

Complaint details

Action (to be) taken
- date completed
- sign-off
- line superior

3. Ensure complaints are assessed correctly

On receipt of a complaint, the recipient should look on it as a second chance to satisfy the customer. Staff should:

- be courteous and empathise with the customer
- ensure that all the details are obtained and recorded on the standard complaints form
- be satisfied that the information is factual
- not admit liability or fault at this stage.

Subject to appropriate information seeking and establishment of the facts, the recipient, in conjunction with his or her line manager if necessary, should decide whether it is a major or minor complaint.

Minor complaints may result from misinterpretation, misunderstanding, detail errors, or straightforward carelessness. Major complaints may involve breach of the criminal law or have health and safety or financial implications.

4. Establish ownership and responsibility

Staff should be empowered to take appropriate action if the complaint is clearly justified, falls within their jurisdiction, and can be rectified immediately. If the complaint cannot be resolved by the recipient, details of the customer and complaint should be noted on the form and passed quickly to the relevant area or level of responsibility. The customer should be told who is dealing with the complaint – nothing is more frustrating than dealing with a faceless organisation, or being passed from one person to another – and that a reply will be given as soon as possible, and within a specified time limit.

5. Establish escalation procedures

In the case of major complaints, the manager should decide on the appropriate action and this may involve:

- consulting a higher authority
- the production of a detailed report on the events
- contact with the organisation's solicitor
- contact with the police.

6. Emphasise customer contact for complaint resolution

If the level of seriousness has been properly understood, and the establishment of the facts correctly carried out, then appropriate action should become apparent. Problem resolution is not a time for negotiation or bartering with a customer who has a genuine grievance and who should perhaps be compensated generously. If there is any delay in resolving complaints, the customer should be contacted at regular, agreed intervals so that a progress update can be given.

7. Ensure complaints forms are signed off

When the problem has been resolved to the satisfaction of the customer, the recipient or superior should sign off the complaints form for subsequent analysis of any complaints trends.

It could be that there is no satisfactory solution, that the customer may require something 'unreasonable' or 'beyond' the remit of the organisation to deliver. If this occurs, it may be appropriate to:

- inform the customer that expectations exceeded capabilities
- re-affirm which steps can be taken
- and to state that a report will be passed on to senior management.

8. Decide internal corrective action

Having dealt with the complaint, decide whether any system, equipment or personnel-related improvement needs tackling. Deal with internal process improvements or training requirements as soon as possible after the complaint has occurred.

9. Build in customer satisfaction checks

After an appropriate interval, say two weeks, get back in touch with the customer to confirm that the complaint was satisfactorily resolved – and to check that the organisation still has a customer.

10. Analyse complaints periodically

All complaints forms should be returned to a simple, central address where a manager should have responsibility for monitoring the level and nature of complaints on a regular basis. The results of this analysis, and details of any corrective action, should be reported to senior management on a regular basis.

Dos and don'ts for handling complaints

Do
- Make customer service part of the corporate culture.
- Empower staff to deal with complaints.
- Keep in contact with the customer to ensure that the complaint is dealt with to their satisfaction.
- Analyse the pattern of complaints and take action to make improvements.
- Treat complaints positively.

Courtesy, speed of response and a personal touch are essential. A complaining customer who gets all three will usually emerge a more satisfied customer than before he/she had any complaints. And he/she will tell others in turn.

Don't allow staff to:
- blame the computer
- say it's not their department
- take the complaint personally or defensively
- allocate blame
- use paperwork to block a fast response to complaints.

Offhandedness, slowness and impersonality are likely to lose you not only that customer but many others as well – bad news spreads.

Useful reading

BOOKS

Dealing with demanding customers: how to turn complaints into opportunities, David M Martin and Institute of Management, London: Pitman, 1994

Tough talking: how to handle awkward situations, David M Martin and Institute of Management, London: Pitman, 1993

JOURNAL ARTICLES

How to handle complaints successfully, Winston Marsh, Australian Accountant, May 1990, pp26–30

Customer-focused re-engineering in Telstra: corporate complaints handling in Australia, Virginia Bendall-Harris Business Change and Re-engineering, Vol 2 no 1, 1994, pp7–14

Employee complaints: act early and be concerned, Henry J Pratt, ARMA Records Management Quarterly, Vol 23 no 1, January 1989, pp26–28

Thought starters

- Do staff know what to do when they receive a complaint?
- Does the organisation receive many complaints?
- Does it receive many different kinds of complaints?
- Are they recorded?
- What happens to the records?
- When you last complained, how was it dealt with? Have you used that organisation again?
- An organisation that never has any complaints is probably a bad one – no one bothers to complain, they just go elsewhere.

Handling the Media

This checklist is designed as an aid for anyone who is required to handle the media – whether it be press, radio or television. The media can be valuable for planting ideas, spreading awareness, selling a product or reputation and gaining competitive advantage, as well as a means of handling a crisis. Successful media contact requires clarity and control. This in turn requires careful planning, preparation and calmness.

Current technology can take an image or remark and broadcast it to millions in minutes; the media can prove a powerful and valuable ally or a devastating force, destroying years of work and trust. Most people come into contact with the media at some time; it is worth remembering Andy Warhol's adage that everyone, at some time, has fifteen minutes of fame. Handling the media, whether proactively or as a reaction to a situation or event, can turn a situation around and create a lasting impression. The media also provide legitimacy for a particular message, and if first impressions count then so do impressions passed on by the media.

MCI Standards

This checklist has relevance for the MCI Management Standards: Key Roles A and B – Manage Activities and Manage Resources.

Definition

The media include any method of broadcasting information, with focus on the press, TV and radio.

Advantages of handling the media effectively

Effective media handling can provide:

- improved sales of a product or service
- greater awareness of a brand
- an enhanced perception of an individual or organisation
- communication of a situation, strategy or plan
- damage limitation in the event of a crisis
- valuable long-term business relationships.

Disadvantages of handling the media ineffectively

Handling the media ineffectively can result in:

- a collapse in confidence
- an end to a profitable business
- a damaged and tarnished reputation, and reduced influence and respect
- confusion, rumour and an incorrect or unfair perception
- missed opportunities.

Action checklist

1. Plan your objectives

Never be rushed in to giving an interview. Decide what you want to achieve and then list no more than five points that you want to get across.

2. Keep it simple and stay in control

Don't assume that the journalist or your audience have the same knowledge and information that you do. Keep the message clear and remember your objectives. It is also important to avoid using jargon or acronyms, and not to patronise.

3. Anticipate likely or difficult questions

As part of your preparation, make sure that you have answers ready for any difficult questions. Don't be afraid of politely challenging questions or assumptions, and make sure that you return to your points and objectives.

4. Be comfortable and relaxed

Prepare yourself before the interview by arriving at the venue early so that you aren't rushed and can familiarise yourself with the surroundings. Talk to the interviewer and check that you are relaxed, prepared and in the right frame of mind. It is also worth checking your appearance as this will certainly influence the interviewer. Breathe deeply, slow down and focus on some relaxed opening sentences and your first main point to get you into the swing of things.

5. Understand the journalist and establish a rapport

It is important to know what the journalist is looking for from the interview so that you can match their requirements with your own. Understand the journalist's motivation and remember that they have a job to do. Although they are unlikely to want to trip you up, they may well do so inadvertently through lack of care, time or preparation. Remember to focus on your main points and use them as the substance to address the questions.

6. Project the right image – and don't be hostile

Be friendly, lively and enthusiastic, but don't put on an act. Convey your personality and your message in your voice. It is important to remain calm and not to become hostile; the reporter really is simply trying to elicit information and not to cross-examine you.

7. Don't tell secrets!

Beware of informal conversations and 'off the record' information. Assume that any information you give to a reporter will be quoted.

8. Cultivate your contacts

Consider generating your own stories and establishing ongoing relationships with the media. The media are frequently undervalued, mistrusted or only used in a crisis: a proactive approach to the media can be of enormous value in establishing understanding and goodwill.

Handling the press interview

1. Newspaper and magazine interviews carry special risks because you rely on the reporter's version of events. Make sure that:

    - you understand each other
    - the facts are correct
    - the reporter understands the story.

2. Find out:

    - the reporter's 'angle' and check that you agree
    - the target audience for the interview
    - whether your rivals will be quoted.

3. Provide good quotes – the written equivalent of the sound bite.

4. Remember that the press likes to present interesting rather than balanced accounts, and telling examples or stories rather than general stories.

5. Ask to see the article before it is printed, and offer to take a call from them later if they want to double-check any point.

6. Remember that journalists are people too. Be nice to them and consider what they want and they will (usually!) be nice to you. Be hostile, defensive or obstructive and you are unlikely to get an empathetic write-up.

Handling the radio interview

1. Preparation

   - Make sure you're on when someone's listening. The best times are 7–9 am, 1–2 pm and 4.30–5.30 pm.
   - If the reporter is coming to you, choose somewhere quiet, unless the background noise adds interest.

2. The interview

   - Be intimate. You're talking to one listener. Choose someone you know and picture them.
   - Avoid abstractions. Use vivid, human examples to paint pictures in the listener's mind.
   - Remember the sound bite. Think up three or four sentences that are particularly quotable and include them, but do avoid repetition of words or phrases which risk causing irritation – unless that is your motive!
   - If you use notes, make them bullet points and don't read from them – audiences can tell.
   - Don't thump the table, crinkle papers, or clink jewellery.

3. Remote studios and phone-ins

   - Assume the microphone is live until told otherwise.
   - Listen hard and take notes if you wish; write down callers' names.
   - Answer when it is your turn.
   - Interrupt when necessary and with confidence, or not at all.
   - Be civil to callers and interviewers, even rude ones, and flatter them – 'That's a fair point, but the real issue here is...'

Handling the TV interview

1. In the studio

   - Dress appropriately: plain colours, no fussy patterns, avoid jewellery.
   - Get used to the environment: arrive early and meet the interviewer.
   - Ask about the line of questioning: what's the first question?
   - If you're offered make-up, take it.

2. On location

   - If you are hosting the crew, find out beforehand what special arrange-ments they need for the shoot.
   - Talk to the reporter(s) as soon as they arrive. Check that you see the situation the same way, and find out whether they need background information.

- Have your own ideas about where you would like to be filmed: consider any distractions and make sure that the background is suitable.

3. During the interview

- Sit comfortably, and be friendly and natural.
- Be serious – smiling can be misunderstood.
- Use positive body language.
- Don't fidget – relax!

Dos and don'ts for handling the media

Do

- Plan your objectives – decide what you want to achieve.
- Find out as much as possible. Who is the audience? What is the media looking for, and what will be the areas of questioning?
- Think about the setting and how you would feel most comfortable.
- Be clear and use friendly, everyday language. Imagine you're talking to an interested stranger at a party.
- Challenge biased questions or incorrect information.
- Relax and be yourself.

Don't

- Patronise or use jargon, and don't smoke.
- Be hostile, abrasive or flustered.
- Be rushed into giving an interview or an answer.
- Assume the interviewer and audience know about you or your subject.
- Ignore the question.
- Be a slave to the question: answer briefly, then say what you want to say.
- Ignore problems. If you feel unhappy, ask to do it again if it's not live.

Useful reading

Tough talking: how to handle awkward situations, David Martin, London: Pitman, 1996
Successful public relations in a week, Claire Austin, London: Hodder & Stoughton, 1992
Media interview technique: handling the media and getting your point across on TV, radio and within your organisation, Peter Tidman, Maidenhead: McGraw Hill, 1992
How to handle media interviews, Andrew Boyd, London: Mercury Books, 1991

Thought starters

- Which media interviews have you seen, heard or read which have impressed you?
- Do you know what the interviewer wants from the interview, and do you understand what is motivating them?
- What are your goals and what outcome are you looking for?
- Are you making the most of the opportunity?

Networking

This checklist is designed to help you to develop your business networking skills, in order to retain and gain customers and suppliers, and to expand your range of beneficial contacts.

MCI Standards

This checklist has relevance for the MCI Management Standards: Key Roles A and B – Manage Activities and Manage Resources.

Definition

The term 'networking' produces different responses from different people. As an activity, networking is not new. It is a well-established activity which has attracted a new label.

Our networks embrace the range of informal and formal relationships in which we are involved; networking implies an awareness of our networks and of their potential value both to ourselves and to other members.

Networks overlap; A and B may be in the same network but each will have contacts in other networks. Our networks are not static – if we use them, they constantly expand, but if we neglect them, they shrink.

Networks are generally of four kinds – personal, organisational, professional and strategic. All provide access to information, development opportunities, support and influence.

Benefits of networking

Networking enables you to:

- improve and extend the quality of your relationships
- create opportunities to meet more potential customers
- be better informed and share information with fellow network members
- share in your customers' social interests, thus enhancing your business relationships
- meet your peers in other organisations.

Disadvantages of networking

Networks don't just happen: they require the investment of those rare commodities, time and energy. They also require a disposition to give as well as take. Most of us are happy to do this; for the minority who are not, networking may be an embarrassment.

Action checklist

1. Prepare for your networking

Networking is an activity and a skill which requires planning if it is to succeed. Remember the aim of networking (in the present context) is to improve your business potential. Spend some time identifying networks of which you would like to be a member. Are you interested in 'talking shops' which may be sources of new contacts, or in situations which may provide opportunities for self-development, or as a step on the road to the development of your business?

2. Identify formal networks and develop relationships with them

Professional Institutes and Associations run local activities and help you to keep up-to-date with technical developments. They inform you about successes and 'best practice' in your line of business and provide support for your continuing professional development.

Trade Associations help you to keep up-to-date with new products and industry trends, and can help to identify opportunities for the future.

Training and Enterprise Councils (TECs)/Local Enterprise Companies (LECs) are bodies with remits to develop training and expertise in their local areas. The objectives of TECs usually include securing the commitment of employers to improve the education and training of their employees and to foster enterprise in the local community. Management Development meetings organised by TECs are usually free of charge, and business expansion advice is also readily available.

Business Links aim to improve the competitiveness of local firms by bringing together local support organisations, such as TECs and Chambers of Commerce, to develop the full range of services focused on customer needs and delivered from a single point of access. Personal Business Advisers will visit you and help you to plan the development and running of your business. Some services are free of charge. Open meetings encourage business people to get together.

Business Clubs are often focused on small businesses, where members have similar ideas and problems. Meetings are usually informal and activities promote contact between members to generate business between them.

Chambers of Industry and Commerce provide information on a wide range of business activities in your area. Chambers have links with Training and Enterprise Councils/Local Enterprise Companies, Business Links and the Department of Trade and Industry. They hold social events to help you establish and build on personal relationships with customers and suppliers. Many local Chambers offer continuous programmes of training courses and seminars.

3. Identify informal networks

These include:

- sports and social clubs
- neighbourhood organisations and community groups
- voluntary organisations.

The range of such organisations varies from town to town and from area to area.

4. Take steps to foster your networks

Consider what networks you belong to and the range of your contacts in each. Who could help you? Whom could you help? Build up a record to which you can refer. Consider how you propose to develop your networks.

Take stock. What do you want from your network? Are you looking for a regular flow of information, opportunities to develop yourself and your business, support, access to influence, or opportunities to become influential? What, in turn, can you contribute? What are you prepared to contribute?

Learn how to behave in ways that are consistent with networking ethics. Be open-minded; keep your promises; treat others in the way in which you would like to be treated; and ask for and give help without embarrassment. Most of all, don't forget to acknowledge help. A smile and a thank-you are beyond price.

How will you go about networking? What style of approach suits you best? Michelli and Straw suggest that there are three styles:

Conscious networkers have clear-cut goals. They recognise what is missing in their networks and set out to identify those who will meet their needs and to meet and develop relationships with them. The approach of conscious networkers is systematic and calculating.

Open networkers are again calculating but tend to take a longer-term view, building networks with the future in mind. Their objectives may be less clear-cut than those of intuitive networkers but they recognise those who may be useful in the future and cultivate relationships with them.

Intuitive networkers are neither systematic nor calculating. They enjoy mixing with people and do so as a matter of course. They are 'good with people' and may even be unaware of the extent of their range of contacts or of their potential value in a business context.

5. Get down to practicalities

● **Design your business card to project you and your business**

Think of all the factors – colour, logo, taste, positive messages – that will help to make people remember your business. There are two sides to your business card, so consider listing some of your services on the reverse side. If you export/import, carry bilingual cards – it will make it easier for your foreign customer/supplier to network with you.

● **Describe your business in a nutshell**

Prepare a clean, short, introductory statement which describes you and your business. If it's more than two sentences long you will lose the listener's attention. Adapt the statement to the person you are talking to – this will prevent it sounding too rehearsed. Use humour if you feel people will be comfortable. It can relax the atmosphere and encourage other people to join in the conversation. But do keep what you have to say brief – no one wants to listen to a long, tedious diatribe about how wonderful your business is. Be brief and let the facts speak for themselves.

● **Prepare a brochure**

If you prepare a brochure describing your products/services, make sure it is in plain English, free from jargon. Clear statements, with plenty of white space, are more effective than a cluttered brochure with lots of colour in it. Remember to convey the message – simply and straightforwardly – that you care about your customers and wish to meet their needs, not just to sell them what you have to offer.

● **Get to meetings/events in good time**

The sooner you get there, the more chance you have to arrange things to your advantage. If there is an opportunity to display your brochures, set out a few for people to pick up. If name badges are available, wear one. Having your own is useful, as event badges often use small print. When you are introduced to new people, let them do the talking to begin with. You will learn about them, what interests them, what is concerning them. Encourage them to talk about their business and their future plans. This information will help you to decide how to develop the new relationship. Don't stay too long with each person. Offer your business card, and suggest you might talk again later. Keep the other person's card in a separate pocket to the one in which you have yours, or you may find yourself handing out someone else's card.

- Offer help

Offer to help if you wish to meet someone again to discuss business. It signals a clear message of service, rather than of blatantly wanting a person's custom.

- Listen to people's contributions

Business presentations at meetings can be ideal for picking up a possible lead – people often express their problems to a group, rather than confide only in their business partners. You may also identify competitors who could benefit from a partnership arrangement.

- Generate a record for each contact

Set some time aside each week to chase up contacts – regular contact with people will encourage them to think about you and possibly steer business in your direction.

- Make notes after informal meetings

You can't easily make notes while talking to people, but you can often jot down a key word which you can expand on afterwards – immediately afterwards, while your memory is still fresh.

Thought starters

- People buy from people, so your customers are part of your network.
- Talk about their problems and how you can help; they don't want to know about yours.
- Recall some point from the last conversation you had with X. It may help X to remember you.

Using the Internet for Business

This checklist provides an outline of the issues associated with using the Internet for business.

MCI Standards

This checklist has relevance for the MCI Management Standards: Key Roles B and D – Manage Resources and Manage Information.

Definition

The Internet is a worldwide network of computer networks, connected to each other by telecommunications links via one of the national backbone networks (such as SuperJanet in the UK). Initially the Internet was used primarily by the military, academics and computer enthusiasts who developed their own code of ethics: that of mutual help and exchange of information. Increasingly commercial organisations are making use of the Internet. The typical Internet user is no longer an 'anorak', nor yet predominantly a 'suit'. Although business use is increasing rapidly, in reality, a wide cross-section of the population is now connected as numbers of users in the UK top 3 million, in the USA 40 million, and worldwide, 60 million.

Benefits of using the Internet

The Internet:

- enables cheap and efficient long-distance communication
- offers unlimited potential for personal networking
- has worldwide marketing potential
- opens up worldwide sources of information
- offers as much security and confidentiality as other communications media
- offers a worldwide common platform for business transactions.

Drawbacks of using the Internet

It:

- still largely only carries information which organisations give away free of charge
- includes information which can be incomplete, illegal, trivial or of questionable quality
- uses only recently developed secure payment systems which are still not yet widely trusted by sellers or buyers
- can be slow, both to connect with and to use
- can be time-consuming and threaten users with information overload.

Action checklist

1. Why bother with the Internet?

Largely because the spirit of the Internet is in tune with current changes in the marketplace and ways of exploring new ways of work. The Internet provides a platform for innovation and creativity, for exploring flexible ways of working, for creating new relationships with new suppliers and customers, and – without getting too carried away – for reaching markets beyond traditional scope.

The Internet is also evolving very rapidly. There is no real evidence for saying that those who leave it late to get on to the Internet will suffer, but latecomers will have a lot of learning, trial, error and experience to catch up with.

2. Familiarise yourself with what the Internet can do

Electronic mail (e-mail) offers a much cheaper and highly effective alternative to sending and receiving messages.

The World Wide Web (WWW) is a medium for disseminating information on a world-wide scale and a forum which is developing for buying and selling. The WWW is a program which cross-references, links and retrieves data from computers around the world, using hypertext which allows you to move from document to document using a mouse to click on highlighted terms or graphics.

Newsgroups and Discussion Lists enable the exchange of ideas with colleagues, known and unknown, all over the world who share the same interests.

File transfer protocol (FTP) allows you to transfer a file held on one computer to another as an alternative to sending it on disk or paper through the post.

3. Explore the relevance of the Internet to your business

Examine the potential of the Internet for reducing costs and increasing the scope and effectiveness of your business in the following areas:

Information gathering and market research: information quality is improving as commercial publishers establish their platforms on the Web. This may be at a price, but will provide the reliability and consistency lacking in the first days of the Web.

Communication and information dissemination: e-mail enables extremely low-cost messaging across borders and time zones to customers, suppliers and partners alike.

Marketing and commercial transactions: as problems of security and confidentiality are overcome, it is likely that an increasing number of commercial transactions will be made on the World Wide Web.

Delivery of services: as well as the possibility of straightforward selling on the Internet, there is also the possibility of delivering added-value services. These may be existing services offered in a new format, such as electronic newspapers or distance-based training courses, or new services specifically created to take advantage of the new medium – at the moment these tend to be consultancy-oriented, such as Web site design, but they are growing and diversifying.

4. Examine the business issues

This means becoming aware of:

The growing area of **Internet law** – especially in the area of intellectual property and copyright. There have already been test cases over the ownership – and therefore rights – of material on Web sites.

Issues of **Security** – such as protecting your information from corruption or the dangers of degradation through hackers and viruses by using firewalls and anti-virus software.

Information overload – seeking measures and procedures which can eliminate the threat of being swamped by the mass of information available through the Newsgroups and the Web.

Issues of **control** – examining the dangers – as well as the potential gain – of providing organisation-wide access to all the services available on the Internet, and deciding who should have access to what.

The possibilities of **buying and selling on the Web** – the WWW is moving beyond its former limits as a marketing device to one where business and financial transactions are becoming the norm. Many major banks and software houses are collaborating on secure financial transactions using various forms of encryption, ensuring that confidential data between buyer and seller travels in safety.

It is predicted to be only a short period of time before exploration of commercial transactions is converted into widespread usage, as confidence spreads.

5. Decide which form of access you require

Large organisations have set up permanent connections to the Internet. This means that their employees enjoy a faster capability for sending and receiving information. Other users access the Internet via a dial-up connection from their PC to a commercial Internet Access Provider. Here the connection is not open all the time but is only activated when the user dials up the Internet Access Provider. This means that email can be sent and received only when the link is open.

Costs of access will vary according to the needs of the subscriber. At the bottom end of the market, an Internet Access Provider will charge around £150 a year for a single simple dial-up connection suitable for the purpose of evaluating the Internet. At the other extreme, full connectivity with very fast connections can run into tens of thousands of pounds; the cost includes a dedicated, leased telecommunications line and maintaining a server for Internet traffic.

6. Develop a strategic approach to Internet operations

A Web site can be fun to design and pack lots of promise into the beginning of an electronic future. However:

- Decide early on how you are going to measure success:
    - by numbers of visitors?
    - by numbers of business enquiries which can be followed up?
    - by cost-savings elsewhere?
    - by direct increase in overall sales?

- Decide who is out there as a potential customer. There are now over 60 million people on the Internet. Categories of users are now being identified through research.

- Decide whether your products or services are suitable for marketing through the Internet. Early research suggests that even traditional manufacturing companies can benefit from taking creative and interactive approaches, such as inviting visitors to design their own car and then test drive it! The major market for development, however, would appear to be in the domain of information services and publications which can be sold on – and through – the Internet.

- Decide what information you want on your Web site and who is to control and update it.

- Decide who in the organisation is to have access. This will largely depend on the culture of the organisation and what kind of grey area exists between trust and supervision. If access is available to all, assess how this might change the information power-base of the organisation. The Internet is a final step in shifting information from a privilege to a working tool which can be acted on – and reacted to – in no time at all.

7. Is the Internet for you?

It is difficult to merely tinker with the Internet. The world is already divided into those who can't live without it and those who can. If the organisation is going to exploit the Internet, it will cost more in terms of exploration and research than first imagined – time and effort are easily absorbed in ever greater quantities. But the Internet will also change the way you work – over time. In the beginning reflect on the:

- liberalisation of information flow which the Internet engenders
- possibilities for flexible working
- skill levels required of staff responsible for Internet operations and training for those who will be using it.

Think of the Internet as a cost-centre of the present and an investment for the future. If commercial gain is a target, then the Internet is unlikely to recoup its costs in the short-term.

Dos and don'ts associated with using the Internet

Do

- Safeguard your computer (especially if it is on a network and if you have a permanent connection to the Internet) against hackers and viruses.
- Ensure that your organisation's use of the Internet is appropriate to its short and long-term objectives.
- Assign the responsibility of the project to somebody who is knowledgeable or is enthusiastic to learn.

Don't

- Forget to monitor all the cost implications.
- Become swayed by the hyperbole.

Useful reading
Understanding business on the Internet in a week, 2nd ed, Bob Norton and Cathy Smith, London: Hodder & Stoughton, 1998
Successful selling on the Internet in a week, Carol O Connor, London: Hodder & Stoughton, 1997
The Internet strategy handbook: lessons from the new frontier of business, Mary J Cronin, Boston, Mass: Harvard Business School Press, 1996

Thought starters

- Has one of your suppliers or customers got an e-mail address?
- Do any of your competitors have a presence on the Internet?

Establishing a Presence on the World Wide Web

This checklist is designed to help those managers considering making information on their organisation, products or services available on the World Wide Web (WWW). It assumes a basic knowledge of the Internet.

The ethos of the Internet was traditionally non-commercial, but it is now an acceptable marketing medium, particularly if some information of value is offered at the same time. The main factor that encourages people to return to a site is the usefulness of the information that is available there; not marketing hype.

MCI Standards

This checklist has relevance for the MCI Management Standards: Key Roles A and B – Manage Activities and Manage Resources.

Definition

The WWW is a system which cross-references, links and retrieves data from computers around the world, using what is called a hypertext system. A piece of software, called a browser, allows users to move from one page to another and one document to another by using a mouse to click on high-lighted terms or graphics. It also allows them to respond to what they see via e-mail links that can be set up. Information can be found in all forms, although text is predominant. A presence on the WWW is achieved by set-ting up documents, each of which has a unique address, known as a uniform resource locator (URL).

Advantages of using the WWW

- It provides another way of advertising.
- You can reach a worldwide audience.
- It enables two-way communication with customers.
- It is open all hours.
- Visits to the site can be monitored.
- It demonstrates that your organisation is up-to-date with modern technology.

Disadvantages of the WWW

- It is impossible to target particular groups.
- Not everybody has access.
- It provides access to such vast quantities of information, much of it of dubious value, that some people tend to avoid it altogether.

Action checklist

1. Work out what you want to achieve

Decide if the WWW is a suitable medium for your business and if so, establish some objectives. Do you want to:

- sign up new customers?
- communicate more easily with existing customers or suppliers?
- steal a march on, or catch up with, your competitors?
- explore and see what happens for a set period, say, 6 months?

2. Look at what others have done

Explore the WWW sites of others, particularly of organisations similar to your own, and see what you like and don't like about them. Look at both the presentation and content of what they offer. Ask yourself if you would be interested enough to return to the site again and again. What lessons do you learn?

3. Decide if you want to host the site yourself ...

Weigh up the benefits of setting up your own communications computer (often called a server) and hosting your own WWW pages against the costs of the hardware and technical resource involved. You will need:

- a computer powerful enough to handle incoming and outgoing traffic
- a router which sends data signals from your network to other networks
- a 'firewall' – a computer which keeps intruders at bay

- a physical cable to the Internet network
- staff to maintain and develop the link and information held at your site.

4. ... or use an Internet Access Provider

Ask questions to establish the following:

- the costs of renting computer space
- arrangements and costs for access to the server for editing and updating
- the provision of user audit trails to identify who is looking at what
- the accessibility, helpfulness and friendliness of the staff
- their ability to speak in layman's language
- how well established the firm is
- who else is using them and for what.

5. Work out how much information you wish to include

Estimate how much you can afford to spend, as the expense of a site is related to its size. Bear in mind how much updating you will need or want to keep your site current and interesting. Work out how the pages can link together to maximise the efficiency of the site: it is unnecessary to duplicate information as the same page can be linked from different places on the site.

6. Register an address for your site

Register an address for your site even if you are not sure that you wish to use the WWW. It costs about £80 for two years (1999 pricing) and can be carried out through an Internet Access Provider. Otherwise you may find that the address which you wish to register has already been taken.

7. Decide if you need any technical or design consultancy

Establish if you have the necessary in-house expertise to construct and design WWW pages to the level of sophistication you desire. If your organisation does not have these skills, decide whether you would prefer staff to develop them or whether you want to outsource the job to a consultant or to the Internet Access Provider if you are using one.

8. Make the site interesting

Ensure that the site is designed with the rules of successful marketing in mind, but also remember that the WWW is a new medium with new requirements and possibilities. Remember the most important points which are to:

- give information of value and not just a marketing description
- make the pages clear, short and to the point
- keep them up-to-date

- create links to other sites of relevance or interest
- build in e-mail links for users.

9. Be sparing with graphics

Be aware that modem users can become frustrated with over-use of graphics. Sophisticated, multi-colour graphics can look great but can also take an age to transmit through the lines, pass through a modem and paint on to the screen. Allow users connecting by modem the choice of dispensing with graphics – even the most simple can take ages to 'come down' the lines.

10. Test the pages

Look at the site on a number of browsers, as a site built for one browser will not necessarily look the same on others. Check the most popular browsers, particularly those produced by Netscape and Microsoft. Ask staff and customers to have a look at the pages and give you some feedback. Did they find them interesting and useful? How easily did they find their way around?

11. Advertise the site

Use advertising mechanisms on the Internet to enable surfers to find your pages:

- official guides
- indexes
- crawlers
- other organisations' sites

as well as all the conventional methods of advertising:

- business cards
- press releases
- mail-shots.

12. Monitor the site

Decide how you will measure success. Will it be:

- the number of visits to the site?
- the number of new customers?
- the level of feedback received?
- the amount of coverage in the press?

Dos and don'ts for establishing a presence on the WWW

Do

- Keep the site updated.
- Make it interesting by providing free information.
- Provide for feedback.
- Remember it is a new marketing medium.

Don't

- Treat the WWW site as just another marketing brochure.
- Launch the site before it is complete.

Useful organisations

These are the telephone numbers of some of the companies offering server space for the WWW.

BTNet	0345 585110
Cix	0181 255 5050
Demon	0181 371 1234
Easynet	0171 681 4321
PSI Net UK:	01223 577167
Pipex	0500 474739

Useful reading

Books

Successful selling on the Internet in a week, Carol O'Connor, London: Hodder & Stoughton, 1997

The world wide web handbook: an HTML guide for users, authors and publishers, Peter Flynn, London: International Thomson Computer Press, 1995

Understanding business on the Internet in a Week, 2nd ed, Bob Norton and Cathy Smith, London: Hodder & Stoughton, 1998

Thought starters

- What has been the best Web site that you have visited? Why?
- Does your organisation produce much information that requires continual updating?
- Do any of your major suppliers/customers/competitors have a presence on the WWW?

Fund Raising

This checklist is a guide for managers handling corporate fund raising for the first time. The economic recession, cuts in government grants and, arguably, the National Lottery have placed enormous demands on corporate charitable funds.

Success in fund raising depends upon a subtle balance of negotiation skills, planning resources and budgets, PR and marketing. Above all it is about building positive relationships with potential funders and convincing them that your cause is the best investment. To be successful, a fund raising appeal must stand out from the crowd and make sound business sense.

MCI Standards

This checklist has relevance for the MCI Management Standards: Key Role B – Manage Resources.

Definition

Fund raising consists of persuading another party to support a requesting organisation by giving money, gifts in kind or other resources which enable the project to happen. The project could be an activity (eg supporting a hospice or a research programme), an item (eg funding equipment for a school or publication of a book) or an event (eg a fun run or a theatre performance).

There are two main types of fund raising:

- Appeals for gifts – support is given freely and the donor receives no benefit (such as membership, tickets to events or advertising). A charity can often claim back tax on these gifts.
- Commercial support – such as sponsorship (eg Carling Premier League) or endorsements/promotions, where the requesting organisation receives a percentage or royalties from the sale of goods or services (eg RSPCA Freedom Foods), or is happy to 'badge' the sponsor's name principally for advertising purposes (eg Embassy World Snooker).

Tax rules vary depending on the set-up, so get advice from an accountant or other financial authority.

Advantages

Fund raising:

- enables a requesting organisation to do something they otherwise couldn't
- has PR benefits – providing a positive public image, targeted at specific sectors if desired
- has marketing benefits – enhancing access to new/specific customers
- has tax benefits – talk to your accountant or finance department
- can boost staff morale through team fund raising or incentive schemes.

Disadvantages

- It takes time and requires resourcing to build contacts and find the right funding option.
- It occasionally creates bad PR – but mostly only when the cause and funder are thoughtlessly matched.

Action Checklist

1. Define the need

Before doing anything it is important to consider whether fund raising is the best course of action. Is it imperative that the project requiring funds goes ahead? Is it the most important priority for funding? If the answer to these questions is 'no', then fund raising may not be the best option.

2. What is the case for funding?

Gather together the most important information about the appeal subject to prove the case for funding. This includes:

- facts – summary explaining what the project is, why it is important and when it needs support
- figures – outline budget explaining funds required and (where possible) those already secured
- the USP (Unique Selling Point) – the factor which is likely to make this project uniquely important to those affected by it, including the potential funder.

3. Examine the funding options

What sort of corporate support will suit your needs? If you are looking to arrange sponsorships and events these often require a mix of skills and resources, for example:

- an **event** needs a venue, ticket administration and insurance
- an **item** needs specialist skills and equipment – publishing a book involves an author, editor, designer, printer, publisher etc
- an **activity** needs target objectives, a plan, programme and costs

No matter how you intend to raise funds, think carefully about everything you want to do and what and whom you need to do it.

- Make a detailed plan – with a proposed programme, costs and objectives
- Think about the resources you will need – people, space and equipment as well as cash. Will you need outside help?

4. Find the right source

Fund raisers should take time to draw up a 'hit list' of companies (or where appropriate) individuals who:

- **might** support the appeal
- **should** support the appeal – they have an interest in the project.

The corporate fund raising pot is not bottomless. Establish right at the start if your project fits the company's funding criteria (and vice versa). If it is company policy to support medical projects, an appeal for arts funding is unlikely to succeed.

Fund raisers and corporate donors will take time to decide who they are happy to link up with. Fund raising involves partnerships so both sides must be comfortable (even if they do sometimes disagree about things!) – for example, environmental charities might choose to avoid companies linked to pollution, and organisations sponsoring rural conservation may well be averse to funding claims from organisations related to genetic engineering.

5. Getting advice

Always ask for advice. This saves a great deal of time sending ill-conceived or unsuitable appeals. Many companies have corporate giving guides or a section in the Annual Report and Accounts which explains company policy and areas of interest. Alternatively, speak to whoever administers the charitable budget, often the Company Secretary. Companies with separate charitable trusts may have a dedicated administrator. Keep your enquiries brief – some administrators deal with hundreds of enquiries a week. Make a **quick** call to find out:

- areas of current interest (some companies always support specific causes, others support a charity for a set period and then move on)
- the date and basic details required to send the request in time for the relevant committee meeting
- whether funds may be available; some companies assign donation budgets 12 months or more in advance.

Speak to any relevant personal contacts – directors or senior managers at the company you are investigating who can be approached for friendly, informal advice – **before** submitting an appeal.

6. Putting together a proposal

By following steps 1 to 5 the correct information to include in the appeal proposal should be available. Keep it short and to the point – unless the company requests specific additional information.

A basic proposal should include a one-side executive summary, a brief budget, objectives and benefits, and elements such as equipment/facilities costs, running costs, salaries and administrative costs. Some companies don't fund salaries or administrative costs – check out the funding policy and make it clear how the project will cover these costs if the corporate donor won't.

7. Meeting the prospect

Invite prospective donors to visit; this provides the opportunity for refining, even improving the proposal. Any donor thinking of giving a significant sum would want to visit the requesting organisation first to make sure the project is viable.

This is a great chance for the requesting organisation to showcase its work. Then both parties can build up a picture to aid decision-making on the project.

A note of warning – charities should be very wary of agreeing to take on a new project simply because it fits in with the donor's wishes. Be flexible, tailor the project to the donor's interests, but fund the work you need to do.

8. Getting a decision

This is usually a case of waiting. Many companies state that if the requesting organisation hears nothing within a specified time they should assume no support will be given. Deciding whether to follow up the appeal with a single well timed call is up to you.

9. Review what happened and plan the future

See what did and didn't work this time and put a plan in place to make things more effective next time. For example:

- was the project clear – does the summary or budget need developing?
- what is the next step with the prospective donor? Can you approach them again later or are they clearly not interested?
- can the prospective donor lead you to other prospects?

It is sensible to build on the relationship established with the donor organisation – in the future they may again be in a position to help. Simple ways to maintain the relationship include:

- keeping the donor informed of how the project is going
- involving them in this/other projects where possible
- making the most of the support with other potential supporters (giving funds is like joining a club).

Dos and don'ts for fund raising

Do

- Conform with the Charities Act. You can get advice on this complex law from the Charities Commission.
- Look for a partnership – even a gift deserves reporting back.
- Understand the benefits to the donor – tax, PR or whatever.
- Say thank you – many recipients don't.

Don't

- Take the money and run.
- Lie – be honest about your campaign or you could end up in court.
- Use the funding for something other than the stated purpose – it is a criminal offence.

Further help

Charity Commission, St Alban's House, 57 Haymarket, London, SW1Y 4QX, Tel: 0171 210 4477

Directory of Social Change, 24 Stephenson Way, London, NW1 2DP, Tel: 0171 209 4949 (Courses), 0171 209 5151 (Publications)

National Council for Voluntary Organisations, Regent's Wharf, All Saints Street, London, N1 9RL, Tel: 0171 713 6161

Thought starters

- Are you aware of the implications the Charities Act has for you?
- What is the unique value of the charitable project you are considering?
- Does the charitable project make financial sense?
- Have you taken advice before the start?

Investing in Your People

This checklist is an introductory guide to applying the Investors In People (IiP) Standard in your organisation.

MCI Standards

This checklist has relevance for the MCI Management Standards: Key Role C – Manage People.

Definition

The goal of IiP is to help organisations develop all their people to achieve business objectives.

Investors in People, a government initiative devised by the Employment Department (now the Department for Education and Employment), is a national standard aimed at helping organisations develop their staff. Resulting from lessons of best practice from organisations in the UK and abroad, IiP is based upon the premise that higher levels of skill and expertise benefit both the individual and the organisation.

Demonstration that the organisation is actively encouraging its employees to develop their skills to achieve business goals is achieved through assessment against the four principles of the national Standard which are described below.

Organisations obtain accreditation as an 'Investor in People' through a process of assessment carried out by the appropriate Training and Enterprise Council (TEC) in England or Wales, Local Enterprise Company (LEC) in Scotland, or Training and Employment Agency in Northern Ireland.

Advantages

Securing the IiP award will:

- demonstrate the organisation's commitment to training and development
- help the organisation in its recruitment and retention practices
- provide a framework for developing the organisation's skill base.

Requirements

There are four principal requirements for achieving the IiP Standard.

1. Public commitment from the top to develop all employees to achieve the organisation's business objectives

There must be a public commitment from the most senior level to develop people. This constitutes far more than a token signature or statement of intent. Commitment must be part of every senior manager's belief system. It needs to be written up in the Strategic Plan, supported by public notices of commitment and reinforced by regular meetings to encourage, support and reassure. The Commitment principle requires that everyone knows the broad aims of the organisation, understands the mission statement – if there is one – and understands that the organisation is committed to their development.

2. Regular reviews of the training and development needs of all employees

IiP requires that training and development needs are regularly reviewed against business objectives and also that a process exists for regularly reviewing the training and development needs of all employees (eg performance appraisal). The organisation should identify the responsibility for developing people (eg line manager or personnel department) and ensure that the resources required to meet the training and development needs are identified in the planning process and made available. The review process also needs to verify that managers are competent to carry out their responsibilities for developing people (eg through their own performance appraisal, by assessment against certain competency standards such as the MCI Standard listed above, or by attainment of a National Vocational Qualification). The review process will include – where possible – the targets and standards set for development actions.

3. Continuing action to train and develop individuals on recruitment and throughout their employment

IiP requires that all new employees are introduced to their workplace effectively and are given the training and development they need to do their job (eg there is an induction programme) and that the skills of existing employees are developed in line with business objectives. IiP requires that all employees are made aware of the development opportunities open to them such as:

- workplace experience
- peer group contacts
- work shadowing
- mentoring
- distance learning
- special projects
- private reading
- coaching
- delegation
- job rotation

- secondment
- a course

- attachment
- sitting-with-Nellie

Effective action should take place – and be seen to be taking place – to achieve the training and development objectives of individuals and the organisation. Managers have a responsibility to encourage and support their employees in identifying and meeting their job-related development needs.

4. Regular evaluation of the investment in training and development to assess achievement and improve its future effectiveness

IiP requires that the organisation evaluates how its development of people is contributing to business goals and targets and whether or not the development actions are effective. The outcomes of training and development should be evaluated at individual, team, and organisational level. The Standard also requires that top management continues its commitment to developing employees and has a clear understanding of the broad costs and benefits of developing people.

Evaluation of training and development activities is clearly difficult when the benefits of certain actions may not be realised until years later. To complete a post-training questionnaire would provide evidence but is often no more than mere tokenism. There are useful ways of evaluation, however, which can be built in to the process:

- at the performance appraisal where value can be recorded
- at team de-briefing sessions
- at de-briefing sessions with line manager or immediate superior.

In attaining these requirements the organisation will need to:

- compile a portfolio of evidence which should demonstrate that actions are being taken to meet the requirements
- send a letter of intent to the local TEC/LEC to register as an organisation undertaking IiP.

The organisation will also need to consider the requirements from the point of view of any major shifts of resources, any significant changes to the way people do things and securing staff involvement and commitment to the Standard.

Action checklist

1. Read the Standard

Try to gain an initial assessment of the implications for your organisation and the whole workforce.

2. Relate the Standard's requirements to your strategic thinking

Ensure that staff training and development are on the strategic agenda, as IiP requires.

3. Appoint a coordinator

Appoint a member of staff as IiP coordinator (this may be from the human resources department).

4. Conduct a training audit

Find out the difference between theory and practice – between what the organisation expects and what is actually happening – in terms of planning and evaluating development activities. Find out what staff really think about the four principal requirements of IiP. Diagnose the gaps between current practice and the Standard's requirements.

5. Produce an action plan for approval

You will find that some aspects of your practice are nearer to the IiP requirements than others. Most of the effort therefore needs to be put into closing these gaps. Much of the resource required will come in terms of time and effort – don't underestimate either.

6. Set up a steering group

Draw the participants from different sections of the organisation to help and encourage with implementation, monitor progress and channel feedback.

7. Make the commitment

This is a formal written commitment to your TEC or LEC to register, usually when you know that you have the staff behind you.

8. Communicate

Hold meetings to explain IiP, the commitment of the organisation, and what it means to departments and individuals. Get the action plan agreed with key people and communicate it to all staff.

9. Plan the training process

Establish a clear and distinct means of planning training and development and evaluating it (eg performance appraisals).

10. Assign and allocate resources

Especially management time, but also an appropriate commitment to a training budget.

11. Build up evidence

The assessor will want to examine written proof of commitment and action as well as visiting your premises to meet the staff. Start to construct a portfolio of evidence which demonstrates that the principles are being adhered to.

12. Check on progress

Build in a regular monitoring process to check that action is taking place as planned and that evidence is being recorded. This should not just be an annual event, but should take place two or three times a year.

13. Prepare a dummy run

Arrange with your IiP advisor for a pre-assessment exercise to learn how near you are to attaining the Standard, or how far away from it. This will help you to prepare for assessment.

14. The assessment

Assessment against the Standard is performed firstly against the portfolio of evidence submitted, and secondly by accredited assessors who come to visit the workplace and interview members of staff on various aspects of the four principles.

15. Post-assessment

Remember that being awarded IiP status is just the beginning; the organisation is periodically re-assessed to ensure that it still meets IiP requirements.

Thought starter

- Is staff development in your organisation haphazard or ad hoc? Or is it structured, flexible and meaningful?

Further *Business Checklists* titles from Hodder & Stoughton and the Institute of Management all at £8.99

0 340 74292 5	Information & Financial Management	❑
0 340 74291 7	Operations & Quality Management	❑
0 340 74288 7	People Management	❑
0 340 74294 1	Personal Effectiveness & Career Development	❑
0 340 74289 5	Personnel Policies, Training & Development	❑
0 340 74293 3	Small Business Management	❑

All Hodder & Stoughton books are available from your local bookshop or can be ordered direct from the publisher. Just tick the titles you want and fill in the form below. Prices and availability subject to change without notice.

To: Hodder & Stoughton Ltd, Cash Sales Department, Bookpoint, 78 Milton Park, Abingdon, Oxon OX14 4TD. If you have a credit card you may order by telephone – 01235 400414
fax – 01235 400454
E-mail address: orders@bookpoint.co.uk

Please enclose a cheque or postal order made payable to Bookpoint Ltd to the value of the cover price and allow the following for postage and packaging:

UK & BFPO: £4.30 for one book; £6.30 for two books; £8.30 for three books.

OVERSEAS & EIRE: £4.80 for one book; £7.10 for 2 or 3 books (surface mail).

Name: ....

Address: ....

....

....

If you would prefer to pay by credit card, please complete:

Please debit my Visa/Mastercard/Diner's Card/American Express (delete as appropriate) card no:

❑ ❑ ❑ ❑ ❑ ❑ ❑ ❑ ❑ ❑ ❑ ❑ ❑ ❑ ❑ ❑

Signature .... Expiry date ....